The Middle of the Night Book

The Middle of the Night Book is dedicated to all young parents who strive to be the best parents they can be. We especially honor the mothers and fathers in the Meld for Young Moms and Meld for Young Dads programs for their commitment to being there for their children, for their desire to learn and grow as parents and for their support of each other.

Meld
parenting that works

Developed and Published by

Meld
parenting that works

219 North Second Street, Suite 200
Minneapolis, Minnesota 55401
(612) 332-7563

Staff
Victoria Hosch
Mary Nelson

Consultants
Ann Walker Smalley
Amy Tomczyk

The foundation of this book came from previous editions
written in 1981 & 1986 by MELD staff Nancy Belbas,
Julienne Smerlinder, and Mary Kay Stranik.

The Middle of the Night Book was
developed with funding support from

The McKnight Foundation and **The 3M Foundation**

We thank them for committing to and believing
in young fathers, mothers, and children.

©1999 Meld

ISBN: 0-9676470-0-2

Those Middle of the Night Questions

The news that you are going to become someone's mom or dad can start a whole lot of new feelings. You may feel excited, afraid, thrilled and more—all at the same time! You begin to look ahead and start to think about what life will be like with your baby.

All of these thoughts, hopes and concerns are perfectly normal. At times when you're waiting for baby to be born, you may find yourself unable to think about anything else. Everything seems to be about that baby! That's great because it's one of the first steps of parenthood—realizing that this baby is a real person and part of your life forever.

But where do you get the information to answer all the questions new parents face? It does seem that the questions come faster and are more pressing in the "middle of the night," when conditions are right for thinking about life ahead.

This up to date book is just for you. It can help answer some of those puzzling questions about babies, baby care and becoming a parent, that occur in the middle of the night or anytime.

Table of Contents

Table of Contents *(continued)*

Table of Contents *(continued)*

© Meld 1999 • 612-332-7563

Chapter 1
Becoming a Parent

Your life is about to change forever. As an expectant parent, you are entering into one of the most challenging and fulfilling adventures you will ever have. To be ready, you need to prepare. This includes taking good care of yourself, thinking and talking about your dreams and fears of parenthood and learning all you can about babies. This chapter helps with ideas for looking ahead to parenting, ways to take care of yourself, things to do to get ready for baby and more.

You're Having a Baby!

This Amazing Time

After the realization sinks in that a baby is on the way, many parents start thinking about the kind of family they want to make for themselves and their child. Thoughts may turn to childhood memories and other past family experiences. Dreams and hopes for the future begin to take on new shape. A good look at the reality of the current situation helps parents make plans to build on strengths and look beyond for additional support and information.

Try writing down your thoughts. Ask family elders to tell you more about your cultural heritage or family history. Find a parent support group to join. Watch other parents caring for and interacting with their children. Do you like what you see? Would you want to be like them as a parent? Take plenty of time to do all this thinking, dreaming and planning. It's the foundation for good decision making and a valuable step in preparing to become someone's dad or mom. After all, loving and caring for your little one will be the most important thing you will ever do.

2

Thinking Back: Family Memories

Taking time to think about your own childhood is an important way to learn more about yourself and what you think about being a parent. It's one of the first steps toward building a family of your own. As your child grows, you will be making choices for your family based on all that happened in the past, what's going on now and your hopes for the future.

Not all memories may be happy ones. Talk to someone you can trust about any that are painful or upsetting. Try to work through what this means to you now. This can be an important part of preparing to be a parent, too.

If you have baby pictures of yourself, add one (or a photocopy) to this page.

What are some early memories of your parents or family? What do you picture when you think back?

_____
_____
_____
_____
_____
_____

Have you heard stories about you when you were a baby?

_____
_____
_____
_____
_____
_____
_____

(continued)

Thinking Back: Family Memories *(continued)*

It can be fun—and informative—to talk with your family about when you were a baby. What memories do they have about you? What do they remember about the place you were born? Who was called to announce your arrival? How were you as a baby—happy or fussy? Sharing these memories can be a time of love and laughter for families as they prepare to welcome and love a new family member.

What do you remember about growing up with your brothers, sisters or cousins?

_____

_____

_____

_____

_____

_____

What family gatherings, traditions and/or celebrations do you remember?

_____

_____

_____

_____

_____

Do you have special memories of things you liked to do with your family as a child?

_____

_____

_____

_____

_____

_____

How did your parents or others show their love for you?

_____

_____

_____

_____

_____

(continued)

Looking Ahead to Being a Parent

What is a mother or father? You probably have a picture of what a "real" parent looks like—and you may not be able to picture yourself in that role! You may picture "real" fathers or mothers as very patient and calm, older, taller—or you may picture none of these things. If you think about it realistically, you will know that parents come in all sizes and shapes, have different personalities and different interests. No two are alike. Talking about what you expect of a parent is one way to prepare yourself for baby and parenthood.

What are your thoughts about your own mother and/or father?

_____

_____

_____

_____

_____

_____

In what ways do you want to be like your own father and/or mother? What do you want to be different?

_____

_____

_____

_____

_____

Are there things you think a mother and/or father must be or must do? Are there things parents never do? Why do you think that?

_____

_____

_____

_____

_____

Are there any people who are parents that you admire? Who and why?

_____

_____

_____

_____

_____

_____

(continued)

Looking Ahead to Being a Parent *(continued)*

What kind of parent do you want to be?

_____
_____
_____
_____
_____
_____

What do you imagine your child will be like?

_____
_____
_____
_____
_____
_____
_____

What do you want to pass on to your child from your family heritage, traditions and/or religious beliefs?

_____
_____
_____
_____
_____
_____
_____

What new traditions do you want to develop for your own family?

_____
_____
_____
_____
_____
_____

6

It Takes Two: The Benefits of Shared Parenting

It helps a child to have both his mother and father involved in his life. Men and women see and experience the world differently from one another. Showing baby both these world-views helps him be better prepared to get along with others. It also helps children understand the opposite sex and how to relate in healthy ways. Involvement with both sides of the extended family—grandparents, aunts, uncles, cousins—enriches a child's life even more.

Parents benefit, too. It helps when the joys and responsibilities of child care can be shared and there is someone to talk to about big choices and everyday challenges. When mom and dad pool their information, strengths, experiences and more, everyone in the family benefits.

Ways Babies Benefit

- Baby benefits when a small, consistent, loving circle of people care for him. Having both parents committed and involved in raising baby often offers better problem-solving, more information and a larger circle of support.

- Children learn about how relationships work from watching others. How feelings are handled, ways family responsibilities are shared and divided, and who is responsible for what, are all lessons learned from watching families.

- When both parents are equally important in baby's life for the routine and ordinary days, as well as for all the wonderful and memorable times, he has the opportunity to compare and contrast his father's reactions with those of his mother. This give emotional balance.

- Baby, above all else, needs to be loved and cared for. How the actual work is divided is of little concern to her. She doesn't really care who changes her diaper. She will learn that everyone pitches in to help because that's what families do.

Ways Parents Benefit

- Expectations for parenthood begin even before pregnancy and continue long after baby is born. When both parents are involved, you can consider any and all opinions, advice and expectations, but will do best when you come up with your own shared parenting plan, one that works for you.

- Parents today have more choices about what kind of father or mother they want to be, but there can be more confusion about those roles, too. Talk about those roles together. Then, make a commitment to be an involved parent.

- Memories of old rules and expectations about parenthood need to be talked about before mothers and fathers can find ways to share the parenting.

- Almost everyone will have an opinion about what makes a "good mother" or a "good father" but it's up to you to decide for yourself what works for you and your family. What matters most is that both parents are able to share in loving and caring for their child.

- Flexibility is important. Moms and dads aren't interchangeable, but each can fill the emotional, social and other needs of their children. They just do it differently.

- When parents disagree they need to listen to each other's view and seek compromise. Teamwork is important.

- Neither parent should change joint decisions once they're made. Be sure decisions are talked through and both parents are in agreement about choices made. Compromise and flexibility are often important parts of these discussions.

- Support or lack of it can affect how well you adjust to shared parenting. Support each other and be committed to the importance of both parents being involved in baby's life.

Shared Parenting: Things to Know

Working out how to share the parenting of your baby can be hard. It may help to think things through while looking at yourself, your child and the situation you are in. Keep in mind that it doesn't really matter what other families do or think you should do. Listen to others and then decide what works best for baby and you.

Know Your Baby

- Baby benefits in many ways from having a family that has found ways to share parenting.

- Baby needs parents who take good care of him, show their love often and in many ways, and who play with, teach and guide him. When parents find good ways to share parenting, baby gets extra love, attention and care.

- No child wants to feel adrift in the stormy sea of daily life. Parents are the anchors that allow children to explore and drift out a little by keeping them safe and loved. Having extra anchors helps a child feel that much safer.

- It may seem ideal for two parents to be in a child's life every day, but that isn't the only way to stay bonded to baby. Noncustodial parents, parents in school, parents who work long hours, parents away for other reasons can still find good ways to create and maintain loving connections with their children.

- Remember, for children actions speak louder than words. Be there for your baby. Share your child by letting others surround her with love and care, too.

Know Yourself

- No one can do everything equally well—there are no "super-parents." Some things must slide, standards may be lowered, whatever. It's up to you to decide where you will spend your best efforts.

- Absent parents miss a lot. They miss regular chances to teach, support and care for their baby. They miss the joys, routines, silliness, milestones and frustrations of baby's life that are so important to building long-lasting, trusting relationships.

- Dads and moms who are committed to working together as they share parenting know that they need to put baby first. Take the long view—there may well be time to do all the things you want, maybe just not today, this week, or even this year. There will be more time for some things as baby grows more independent.

Know the Situation

- Jobs, school, health, experience, stress and more all effect how parents share caring for baby. Find someone who can help you think and talk through ways to solve problems that get in the way of sharing parenting. Your baby needs you in her life.

- How we choose to spend our time may interfere with our focus on sharing parenting. Volunteer activities, playing sports or hanging out with friends are all important and healthy choices, but keep things in balance by remembering baby's needs, too. Remember, you're the most important person in your baby's life.

8

A Commitment to Shared Parenting

Shared parenting means sharing the responsibilities and decisions of raising your baby. This can be difficult to do when two parents live together and it can be even tougher when they don't. The key to successful shared parenting is to talk about the issues and work out the best way to do things—a way that considers both parents' and baby's needs. Shared parenting requires communication, flexibility, compromise, commitment and agreement. It helps to remember to always put baby first. Using this page can help you work out ways to share parenting. One of the first steps is to make a commitment to being a good parent. The next step is to recognize and accept parenting responsibilities and then decide how each parent will make shared parenting work for them and their little one.

My commitment to my baby:

❏ Being a parent is my #1 priority. My baby comes first in all choices I make.

❏ If I say I'll do something for my baby, I can be counted on to do it.

❏ I know my child will benefit from having both parents in his life. I will work to try to make that happen.

❏ Other: _____

_____

_____

My responsibilities as a parent is to:

❏ Maintain my own physical and emotional health and safety.

❏ Communicate with my baby's other parent about our child.

❏ Take care of baby's physical needs (food, clothing, cleanliness, shelter…)

❏ To take care of my child's health (medical care, immunizations, childproofing…)

❏ Create a safe and healthy environment for my child. This includes knowing the people who visit my home and those who care for my child, keeping drugs, alcohol, and other substances away from my child, keeping guns and other dangerous items locked up, avoiding risky behaviors myself, maintaining healthy relationships and more.

❏ Talk about and work out custody and visitation plans.

❏ Encourage baby's healthy growth and development by providing appropriate activities, self-esteem boosts, play, exploration, friendships and more.

❏ Take care of my baby financially now and in the future.

❏ Help educate my child now and in the future.

❏ Pass on to my child her family heritage.

❏ Be flexible and willing to compromise with my baby's other parent.

❏ Other: _____

_____

_____

I respect and value my commitment to being the best parent I can be. I will be faithful to my child and to working out ways to share the responsibilities of parenting

Signed: _____

Shared Parenting: We Can Work It Out

Once each parent understands and accepts the responsibilities and commitments they have made to their child, you can begin to decide how the actual "work" of parenting will be shared.

Now that I am a parent, this is how I will:

❑ **Maintain my own physical and emotional health and safety.** Avoid risky behaviors, no drinking or drugs, get medical care as needed, no guns in my life and more.

_____

_____

_____

_____

_____

❑ **Communicate with my baby's other parent.** Talk about what is happening with baby, discuss decisions that need to be made and more.

_____

_____

_____

_____

_____

❑ **Take care of my child's physical needs (food, clothing, cleanliness, shelter, etc.).** Decide who will do what part in providing for child's physical needs, where child will live, who will buy which clothing and more.

_____

_____

_____

_____

_____

❑ **Take care of my baby's health (medical care, immunizations, childproofing, etc.).** Decide how we will share responsibility for getting baby to doctor for well-child checkups, who will take sick baby to doctor, how home(s) will be childproofed and more.

_____

_____

_____

_____

_____

(continued)

10

Shared Parenting: We Can Work It Out *(continued)*

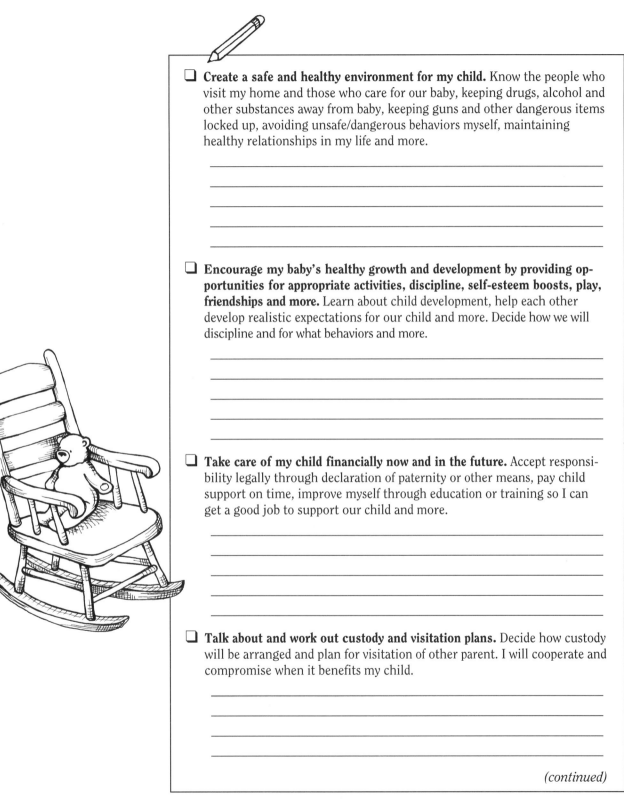

❑ **Create a safe and healthy environment for my child.** Know the people who visit my home and those who care for our baby, keeping drugs, alcohol and other substances away from baby, keeping guns and other dangerous items locked up, avoiding unsafe/dangerous behaviors myself, maintaining healthy relationships in my life and more.

_____

_____

_____

_____

_____

❑ **Encourage my baby's healthy growth and development by providing opportunities for appropriate activities, discipline, self-esteem boosts, play, friendships and more.** Learn about child development, help each other develop realistic expectations for our child and more. Decide how we will discipline and for what behaviors and more.

_____

_____

_____

_____

_____

❑ **Take care of my child financially now and in the future.** Accept responsibility legally through declaration of paternity or other means, pay child support on time, improve myself through education or training so I can get a good job to support our child and more.

_____

_____

_____

_____

❑ **Talk about and work out custody and visitation plans.** Decide how custody will be arranged and plan for visitation of other parent. I will cooperate and compromise when it benefits my child.

_____

_____

_____

_____

(continued)

Shared Parenting: We Can Work It Out *(continued)*

❑ **Help educate my child now and in the future.** I will help my baby grow and learn right from the start. I will, in the future, participate in my child's school life, help with homework, go to school meetings and other things as needed. I will plan for and encourage my child's further education as he gets older.

_____

_____

_____

_____

❑ **I will be flexible and willing to compromise with my baby's other parent.** I will talk to my child's other parent if changes need to be made in the schedule or if other things change. I won't rigidly stick to our agreements, if change is possible that benefits our child.

_____

_____

_____

_____

❑ **Pass on to my child her heritage (cultural, religious and more).** Decide how my child will be taught religion, which language she will speak (if appropriate), make sure she knows her relatives, help her understand her ethnic background and more.

_____

_____

_____

_____

My child's other parent and I are willing to meet half way about things we still don't agree on, including:

_____

_____

_____

_____

_____

_____

_____

Real Parents/Real Issues

It can take a lot of time and a lot of discussion to get plans to the point that everything is working for a family. Here are some ideas to try as you determine how you share parenting.

What's Up?

When it comes to shared parenting it's helpful to identify the things that are most important to you. Know what you expect and why. Think about the role you imagined for yourself. Decide what can be changed and where you're not so flexible. Minor tensions and misunderstandings can become big issues if not identified and worked out.

Talk It Out

Good communication includes a willingness to talk and listen. Think about what you want to say, pick a good time to talk, be committed to listening and plan on being flexible. Keep in mind that as time goes on, things change for you and for baby. These changes mean that parents need to keep communication open and be willing to adapt. A sense of humor helps too—laughing with another is a great way to diffuse tension and move on.

Rethink Roles

Some problems that come up may be caused by differing ideas about the roles of men and women, mothers and fathers. Discuss your expectations and look for ways to compromise. Try new ways of doing things if that will help your new family.

Don't Worry What Others Think

Society—including relatives, friends, neighbors—has its own set of expectations for men and women. Parents interested in trying new roles that may work better for them can't afford to worry too much about what others think.

Be a Team

Babies and parents benefit when both mom and dad work out ways to share parenting and to be a team for their child. Be clear about who will do what when it comes to caring for baby. It doesn't have to be a 50/50 division of labor, but it does need to be shared so that both parents feel OK about their opportunities and responsibilities.

Grandparents

Grandparents and others can welcome a new child with such enthusiasm that they can overwhelm new parents. Recognize their joy and desire to help, but if necessary, talk to them about setting limits on their advice before it becomes "interference." Also understand, that in some states, grandparents can file for legal visitation rights. Try to find good ways to communicate with and involve all your child's grandparents in her life whenever possible. In most instances, everyone benefits—grandparents, parents and baby!

Parent Care

Even though you're a parent 24 hours a day, you still need time just for you. You have a life beyond parenthood that you need to maintain and nurture for your physical, spiritual and emotional well-being. Think about what energizes or relaxes you. Make a plan for ways to take time for these activities regularly. Take time to care for yourself so you have what it takes to be the best parent you can be. Remember, baby needs you.

Building Your Village: Finding Help and Support

Facing parenthood for the first time can be a whirl of emotions and worries. Finding people to talk to and who will support you in your decisions can help you work through your worries and fears. You don't have to do it all alone. Just as it takes a village to raise a child, that same "village" can be there to help parents. Build your village by looking around you at family, friends and others who are there to circle you with support.

Here are some places to look for help and support. Use the following worksheet to see who you can identify as part of your "village" or support circle. Keep their phone numbers handy for when you need to talk.

Baby's Other Parent

Sharing your fears about the birth and parenthood, your hopes and dreams for your child's future, and how you hope to raise your baby can help you prepare for parenthood. Support each other in this new challenge to be the parents your baby needs and deserves.

Your Family

Family members can be a great source of love, help and advice. They often have experience with different ages of children, different personalities and more. Seek their advice—they may give it anyway—and use it to help your family grow.

Parenting Groups

Many communities sponsor groups for parents to get together and discuss issues faced by all parents. Some groups are organized by the age of the child, others by neighborhood, or around an issue, like discipline. Support groups give parents a chance to meet others who are facing similar situations. These groups are good places to make new friends and they offer more chances to develop your circle of support.

Those Around You

Look around at all the parents you know. It could be friends, relatives, neighbors, others. Which ones are the kind of parent you want to be? Talk to them about what parenting is like. You might pick up some tips and good advice.

Some Final Thoughts

It's important to nurture the support and help of others by letting the person know how they helped and how much it meant to you. Don't forget to give something back. One of the best ways to build your village of support is with a willingness to help someone else build theirs.

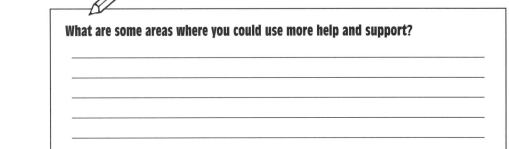

What are some areas where you could use more help and support?

_____

_____

_____

_____

_____

_____

(continued)

Building Your Village: Finding Help and Support *(continued)*

Take a look around at all those people who surround you with help and support. Put their names around the circle. List their phone numbers on the next page so you have them handy when you need to call.

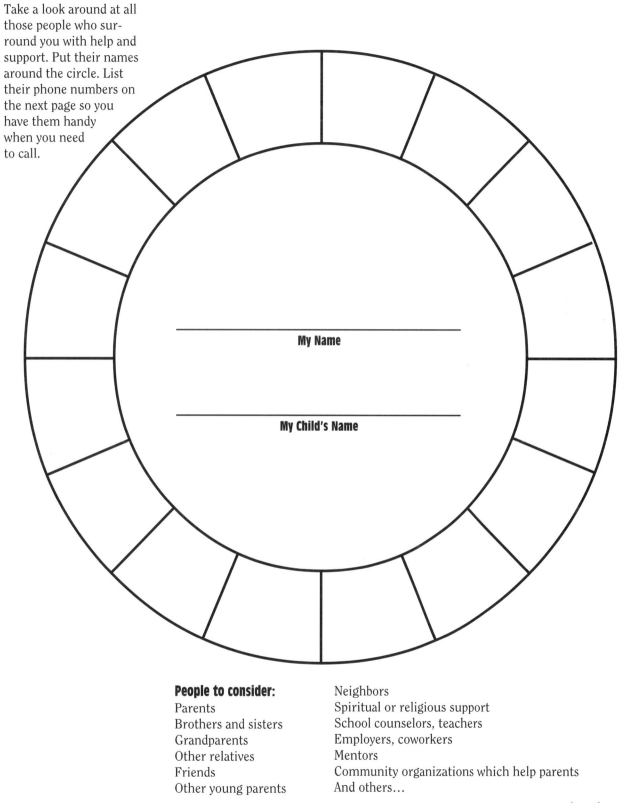

_____

My Name

_____

My Child's Name

People to consider:
Parents
Brothers and sisters
Grandparents
Other relatives
Friends
Other young parents

Neighbors
Spiritual or religious support
School counselors, teachers
Employers, coworkers
Mentors
Community organizations which help parents
And others…

(continued)

Building Your Village: Finding Help and Support *(continued)*

Support Circle Phone Numbers

Family _____
_____
_____
_____
_____
_____

Friends _____
_____
_____
_____
_____

Others who care _____
_____
_____
_____
_____
_____

Groups and
organizations _____
that help parents _____
_____
_____
_____

Others _____
_____
_____
_____
_____

 16

Chapter 2
Nine Months Long

We hope that all expectant parents are signed up for child birth classes. These can be a great source of information and support for both parents. You will learn what to expect during labor and delivery, what will happen in the hospital and more. The class is a good place to get questions answered, too. Check with your doctor for classes near you.

Preparing for the birth of a new baby can be an exciting time. To be ready for this important event, mothers and fathers need to take care of themselves. This includes eating and resting well, exercising, sharing your dreams and fears of parenthood, planning, learning, thinking and probably even worrying—just not too much. This chapter will help you get ready for baby. It gives information about prenatal health care, baby supplies to get ahead of time, hospital plans and more.

What's Going On In There? Mom and Baby Develop

It's amazing how quickly you will notice differences in mom's body as it changes with the developing baby. Some changes are visible to the rest of the world. Others are more inside—how mom feels, body temperature changes, lack of menstruation. As these changes happen, mom may feel mildly uncomfortable at first and wildly uncomfortable by the end of the pregnancy! Not all women react the same to pregnancy—some have morning sickness, others don't. Some gain a lot of weight right away; for others it may take longer. Some of the changes go away after awhile, like morning sickness, while others stay with mom the whole nine months, like the need to go the bathroom all the time. Whatever changes take place, all moms and dads need love and support in this exciting time.

The First Three Months

Baby's Development	Mom's Body Changes and Hints
One Month: • 1/4" long • Curved like a bean • Heart starts to beat • Arms and legs sprout • Eyes and brain begin to develop **Two Months:** • One inch long, 1-1/2 oz. in weight • Human appearance • Muscles forming • Eyelids form • Baby's gender can be determined • Smooth movements • Hair on head • Has fingers and toes • Beginnings of teeth	**Mom may feel tired. Her body is adjusting to the changes and using a lot of energy for baby's growth.** Rest when possible and get more sleep at night. **Upset stomach, especially in morning. Body chemistry changes due to pregnancy and rapid growth of baby upsets mom's system.** Keep stomach filled with many small meals, especially protein snacks (milk, cheese, peanut butter). Try nibbling soda crackers. Avoid greasy or spicy foods. Keep up normal activity to keep mind off nausea. **Need to go to the bathroom more often because baby is resting on mom's bladder.** Wherever you go, know where the bathrooms are! Don't cut back on liquids, though, because your body needs the fluids. **Breasts starting to get ready to feed baby. They may feel tender, nipples may darken and area around nipples may have tiny bumps and may leak whitish fluid.** Try a larger size, more supportive bra. Many women wear one 24 hours a day. If nipples leak, rinse with water, wear absorbent liners in bra cups. **Body temperature rises because mom's body is working harder for her and baby.** Dress in removable layers of clothing. **Mood swings due to changes in body chemistry and because having a baby is a lot to think about!** Talk about feelings with someone. *(continued)*

The Middle Months

Baby's Development	Mom's Body Changes and Hints
• 12" long, 1/2 to one pound in weight • Mom can feel baby move • Fine hair covers whole body • Rapid growth • Complete finger-nails and eye-lashes • Ears, nose and mouth • Heartbeat can be heard	**Mom's appetite returns and she gains weight more quickly—about a pound a week as baby grows.** Eat healthy meals and snacks. Mom's body will tell her when and how much to eat. **Mom begins to "look pregnant" and stretch marks may appear on her stomach as baby gets bigger and bigger.** Wear looser fitting clothes. Lotions to soften skin may relieve itching and help skin stretch. **Backaches are common because larger tummy puts strain on back.** Wear shoes with low heels. Use a foot stool when sitting. Lean forward (over a table or kitchen counter) to relieve back pressure. Mom can lie on her side. Use pillows to support body wherever it feels comfortable. **Vaginal discharge (a white discharge on under-wear) due to hormonal changes.** Bathe frequently; wear mini-pads. If there is itching, burning or a bad odor, check with your doctor. There may be infection.

(continued)

The Last Three Months

Baby's Development	Mom's Body Changes and Hints
• 19" to 21" long, 6 to 8-1/2 pounds in weight • Baby is fully developed • Baby's head drops into mom's pelvis • Weight gain about 1/2 pound per week • Eyes are slate colored—not final color	**Heartburn and indigestion due to sluggish stomach.** Eat smaller amounts of food more often. Avoid greasy foods. **Varicose veins (enlarged veins on legs) caused by the pressure of the growing baby.** Lie down, put legs up. Wear support hose. **Constipation occurs because mom's uterus is enlarged causing crowded bowels to move more slowly. Hemorrhoids happen because of enlarged blood vessels. Black stools are caused by the iron supplements mom may take.** Drink eight glasses of water daily. Eat high fiber and fresh foods. Take warm baths. Iron reaction isn't harmful and is only temporary—nothing needs to be done. **Swelling of legs and ankles because body retains fluid.** Sit instead of standing. Lie down instead of sitting. May need to reduce salt in foods. **Sleeping may become more difficult as baby's activity and size increase. Mom may have trouble finding a comfortable sleeping position.** Take a walk before bedtime. A warm bath may help or practice relaxation techniques. Use extra pillows to support pelvic weight.

Danger Signals During Pregnancy

Most women won't have any of these signs, but if you do call your doctor immediately:

• Vaginal bleeding

• Sharp, constant stomach pain

• Gush of water from vagina

• Painful, continuous headache, especially after week 20

• Blurred or double vision or spots before mom's eyes

• Fever over 100° F and chills

• Swelling of face, hands and feet

• Burning and pain when urinating

• Severe, continuous vomiting

• After the fifth month, if baby shows no movement for 12 hours

Eating for Two

Healthy eating for both mom and baby is important because what mom eats is what baby "eats." If mom eats junk food in place of nutritious food, baby won't get the what he needs to grow strong and healthy. Look over these suggestions and those of your doctor for healthy eating during pregnancy. Baby's dad can help by encouraging mom to eat well and by avoiding junk foods himself.

Choose at least one serving daily from the Vitamin C group and one from the Vitamin A group for both fruits and vegetables.

Food Group	Daily Number of Servings	One Serving is...	What It Provides Mom and Baby
Milk Whole, skim, 2%, fresh, powdered, evaporated **Other Milk Products:** cottage cheese, yellow cheese, ice cream, yogurt and other foods made with milk.	4 to 5 servings	• 8 oz. glass of milk • 1 cup cottage cheese • 1 cup ice cream • 1-1/2 slices cheese • 1 cup yogurt • 1 cup pudding	**Calcium:** builds bones, teeth, helps nerves and muscles work well. **Protein:** builds body, brain, blood. **Vitamin A:** for eyes, skin, hair and normal body growth.
Meats and Other Proteins Red meat (like beef and pork), fish, chicken, eggs, chitlins and menudo. Also, pinto beans, dried peas, nuts, soybeans and peanut butter.	2 to 3 servings	• 2 to 3 oz. of meat (about the size of the back of your hand) • 2 eggs • 1 cup cooked beans • 2 tbsp. peanut butter • 1/2 cup nuts • 1 cup dried peas/beans • 1 cup tofu	**Protein:** builds body, brain, blood. **Iron:** for red blood cells, prevents anemia before and after birth. **B Vitamins:** to help body use iron, for healthy nerves and good appetite.
Fruits For **Vitamin C:** oranges, lemons, grapefruit, strawberries, apples. For **Vitamin A:** cantaloupe, plums, peaches, blueberries.	3 to 4 servings	• 1/2 cup cooked or canned fruit • 2 tbsp. dried fruit • 1 cup raw fruit • 1 piece fruit • 3/4 cup strawberries • 1-1/4 cup watermelon • 1 cup orange juice	**Vitamin C:** helps keep body healthy; needed for teeth, gums, bones, body cells and blood vessels. **Vitamin A:** for eyes, skin, hair and normal body growth.

(Continued)

Eating for Two *(continued)*

Mom's Weight Gain During Pregnancy

- Plan to gain 25 to 35 pounds. Expect to gain two to four pounds over the first three months and slightly less than one pound a week after that.

- Eat foods from each food group. Take vitamins and iron supplements if doctor recommends them. Mom must eat right so baby gets the right proteins, minerals and vitamins he needs in order to grow.

- Never try to lose weight during pregnancy. Baby will be small and have a greater chance of being sick or dying early in life if mom diets to lose weight while pregnant.

- See doctor if there is sudden weight gain—like five to ten pounds in one week.

- Don't worry about losing weight after delivery. It takes a week or more to lose the first 12 to 15 pounds. Mom will lose the next 12 to 15 pounds in the first six weeks.

- Breastfeeding baby helps mom's uterus return to it's previous size and often helps with weight loss.

- Taking 400 micrograms of folic acid every day may reduce a woman's risk of having a child with a birth defect.

Food Group	Daily Number of Servings	One Serving is...	What It Provides Mom and Baby
Vegetables For **Vitamin A:** green or red chiles, carrots, spinach, greens, pumpkins, any dark yellow or dark green vegetables. For **Vitamin C:** tomatoes, brussel sprouts, broccoli, green chile, potatoes.	3 to 5 servings	• 1 cup broccoli • 1/2 cup carrots • 1/2 cup squash • 1/2 cup green beans • 1/2 baked potato • 1 medium tomato • 1 cup collard greens, kale or cabbage	**Vitamins A and C:** For good looks — eyes, skin, hair and normal body growth.
Breads and Cereals whole grain or "enriched" bread, fortified breakfast cereals, muffins, tortillas, fried bread, buns, rice, macaroni.	6 to 11 servings	• 1/2 cup cooked cereal • 3/4 cup dry cereal • 1 slice bread • 1 large tortilla • 1/2 cup cooked noodles, rice or macaroni • 1 bun or biscuit • 1 pancake • 4 soda crackers	**B Vitamins:** For healthy nerves, good appetite and helps body use other nutrients. **Iron:** for red blood cells, prevents anemia before and after birth.
Water	6 to 8 glasses		**Body fluids:** helps the body use the foods and carry wastes out of the body.

Taking Care of You Takes Care of Baby

Baby is counting on you to help her grow healthy and strong, even before she is born. Parents make a big difference in how healthy a baby is by eating well and avoiding foods and substances which can harm baby. Dad and others help in additional ways by encouraging and supporting mom to keep making healthy choices.

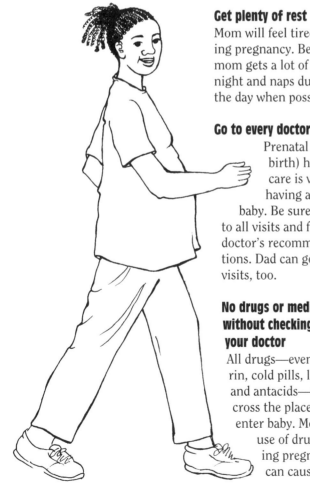

Eat well and avoid junk food

A poor diet can cause problems for parents and baby, both mentally and physically.

Pregnant moms should only eat well-cooked meat during pregnancy

Don't eat raw or under-cooked meat, fish, poultry or eggs. These can have germs that can make mom and baby sick.

Get plenty of rest

Mom will feel tired during pregnancy. Be sure mom gets a lot of rest at night and naps during the day when possible.

Go to every doctor visit

Prenatal (before birth) health care is vital to having a healthy baby. Be sure to go to all visits and follow doctor's recommendations. Dad can go to the visits, too.

No drugs or medications without checking with your doctor

All drugs—even aspirin, cold pills, laxatives and antacids—will cross the placenta and enter baby. Mom's use of drugs during pregnancy can cause baby to be born addicted to the drug. Dad can help by encouraging mom and avoiding drugs himself.

No smoking

Smoking can cause babies to be born too small or too soon. Small babies have a higher risk of dying early in life. These dangerous effects are directly linked to the **number** of cigarettes a mom smokes daily. Secondhand smoke from dad or others can hurt baby, too.

No beer, wine and hard liquors

Drinks during pregnancy risks damage to baby's brain and growth. Since doctors aren't sure exactly how much drinking is dangerous, the best choice is to avoid drinking completely. Dad can help by avoiding these drinks, too.

Avoid x-rays

Stomach or back x-rays may cause damage to baby. Always tell your doctor or dentist you are pregnant.

Only small amounts of colas, tea, coffee or chocolate

These all contain caffeine. Large amounts have been found to cause birth defects in unborn animals.

Stay away from sick people

Some diseases, like rubella or German measles, Fifth's disease and CMV can cause damage to an unborn baby. Tell your doctor if you have been exposed to any serious illness.

Let doctor know about STDs

(genital herpes, HIV/AIDS, chlamydia, gonorrhea or other sexually transmitted diseases) Report **any** symptoms which occur. An active infection at the time of baby's birth can cause blindness, pneumonia or other infections for the baby unless preventive steps are taken.

Do not empty the cat's litter box; have someone else clean it

Cat waste can harbor an infectious disease that can cause birth defects.

Scrub all fruits and vegetables before eating or cooking

Wash your hands frequently

Germs are easily passed hand-to-hand. Keep your's clean.

© Meld 1999 • 612-332-7563

What to Expect at Prenatal Visits

Expectant parents can plan on the these basics at a typical prenatal visit. Your doctor may offer care that is somewhat different. If you have any questions, be sure to ask. Remember, it's your right and responsibility to understand the care provided for you and your baby.

Frequency of appointments
- Once a month for the first seven months
- About twice a month for the two months before the birth
- Weekly when close to the due date
- More often if problems arise
- Immediately if danger signs appear

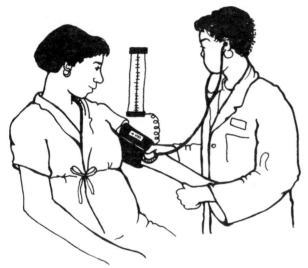

Questions asked
The doctor or nurse will ask questions to put together a personal and family health history to calculate the due date and whether the pregnancy carries any risks for the baby or mother. The doctor or nurse may ask questions like these:
- Date of last menstrual period?

- Has there been any bleeding?
- Has mom used any alcohol or drugs during pregnancy?
- History of other pregnancies, miscarriages, premature deliveries, etc.
- If your blood type is RH-negative and other parent's blood type RH-positive.
- Has there been exposure to an infectious disease or STD? Has mother had a urinary tract infection?
- Any history of diabetes or thyroid problems in either family?
- Any family genetic problems or diseases? Most genetic problems will not affect pregnancy or childbirth, but will alert the doctor to take certain health steps.

Blood pressure
Mother's blood pressure will be taken and recorded at each visit.

Weight gain
Keeping track of how much and when weight is gained during pregnancy is important and will be done at each visit.

If mom is not gaining enough weight, baby may be too small. If too much weight is gained, there may be concern about a balanced diet or about mom's energy level and the amount of exercise she's getting.

Lab tests
Mom's urine will be tested for sugar levels and for signs of infection. Blood samples will be taken to test for anemia, STDs/HIV and blood type.

Pelvic exams
The health care provider will use instruments which allow her to take a pap smear and to look at the cervix and pelvic areas. The pelvic exam will be done at the first appointment and at a few other times during the pregnancy.

Your questions
Both parents will have questions for the doctor or nurse. Before the appointment, write down your questions and bring them with you so you can record the answers and write other notes.

24

Is Breastfeeding or Bottle-feeding Right for You?

Before baby is born is the time to decide how you plan to feed baby. Either breast or bottle-feeding will give baby the nutrients he needs to survive and thrive. Discuss the issue and make a decision so you are prepared to begin feeding baby in your chosen way in the hospital. Keep in mind that no matter how you feed baby, feeding time is about more than food. It's a special time when baby and parent can feel extra close as baby snuggles in with those he loves most.

It is important to know that the American Academy of Pediatrics says that breast milk is the most perfect food for babies. They recommend breastfeeding for the first year.

For more information about breastfeeding or if you need help and support once you start, talk to your doctor. It may also help to call the LaLeche League at 1-800-368-4404. This group encourages breastfeeding by offering one-to-one help and can answer questions you might have.

Advantages of Breastfeeding	Advantages of Bottle-feeding
Emotions and Attachment Baby gets closeness and cuddling from being held.	Baby gets closeness and cuddling from being held.
Nutrition • Contains the perfect nutrients. • Is clean, free of impurities. • Is more rapidly and thoroughly digested than formula. • Protects baby against infections, allergies and illnesses by building baby's immune system. • Changes as baby grows.	• Is a complete infant food. • Is patterned after breast milk.
Preparation Breastfeeding requires no preparation. It's always ready for baby. No mixing, no clean up, no trips to the store!	Premixed, ready-to-serve formula is fairly easy to use. Powdered or concentrated formulas are easy to mix. Follow the directions when adding water so it has the proper food value. Bottles and nipples must be washed and formula bought and stored.
Flexibility Mom doesn't need to feel tied down. She can provide bottle-feedings by pumping breast milk or several times a week, formula can be offered.	Others can easily feed baby at any time.
Cost Very inexpensive. Only real cost is for mom's extra good nutrition. This is essential. Baby will not get what she needs unless mom is eating well.	Costs vary but are relatively inexpensive if you use powdered formula. Premixed and ready-to-serve formula is more expensive.
More: • Breastfed babies are healthier (fewer ear infections, colic, upset tummys and other problems). • When parents breastfeed they are less likely to overfeed baby. • Breastfeeding helps with weight loss and causes uterus to more quickly return to it's regular size.	• Bottle-feeding helps parents exactly know how much baby eats. • Parents who bottle-feed can be in any physical condition and still feed baby adequately.

Baby Stuff: Equipment

There are many, many styles and types of baby equipment. It's easy to be overwhelmed by the choice and the variety. It's also easy to convince yourself that baby needs it all! There are only a few things that baby must have—a car seat is one—but there are a few other things that might make life easier and more comfortable for parents and baby. Consider getting just the basics for now and adding other items as baby grows. When buying or borrowing any equipment, always put safety first.

Many communities have car seats available for loan or at low cost. Your child birth class instructor, doctor or clinic may know where to find these car seats.

Needed

Bed

All babies need a safe place to sleep. For the first two years a crib can meet this requirement. When buying (or borrowing) a crib be sure it meets these safety standards:

- Slats must be less than 2-3/8" apart (about three fingers wide)
- No cutouts in headboard or footboard that could trap baby's head
- Corner posts should be not more than 1/16" above end panel to prevent tangling of clothing around neck
- Crib mattress should fit snugly so that two adult fingers cannot fit between mattress and crib side
- Drop-side latches should securely hold sides up.
- All screws, bolts and other hardware should be smooth, free of sharp edges

Other sleeping options

Newborn infants may sleep in a safe, padded cardboard box, a laundry basket, even a dresser drawer on the floor. As baby grows, he will need a larger, safe place to sleep.

Infant car seat

Every infant (and child up to 40 pounds) who rides in a car must be in a federally-approved safety car seat. Buy or borrow one before baby is born for a safe ride home from the hospital. Every brand of car seat installs differently; be sure you understand how to use the one you have. This is important. An incorrectly installed car seat won't protect baby!

Choose either an infant-only car seat or a convertible seat for infants/toddlers. An infant-only seat is designed to face the rear in a reclining position. It fits infants and babies up to 20 pounds. The convertible seat, for babies from birth up to 40 pounds, can be used in the rear facing reclining position at birth and then turned around in an upright, forward position when your child weighs 20 pounds. Find the seat that works best with your car.

And remember, whichever car seat you use, kids always sit in the back seat.

(continued)

Recommended

Changing area

A changing table can make diaper changes easier on parents' backs because it's taller than an average table. A changing table needs safety straps to prevent falls and shelves or drawers that are easily accessible without leaving baby alone on the table. You can use a padded chest of drawers, the crib or even the floor instead of a changing table.

Diaper pail

Cloth or disposable, you still need someplace to put the dirty ones. Look for a diaper pail or container with a tight-fitting lid.

Stroller

There are many styles of strollers—everything from big strollers with baskets, cup holders and other accessories to smaller lightweight models. Look at when and where you will most use the stroller and then test a variety until you find one that meets your needs.

Highchair

Around six months, baby can sit up and eat solid food. A high chair is a safe place to feed him. He can sit securely while you feed him and also enjoy finger foods on the tray of the chair.

Nice, but not necessary

Rocking chair

A good way to soothe a crying baby.

Baby bath tub

Some are designed to fit into a sink or bathtub Others are made to be placed on counter tops or the floor. They come in different sizes and shapes. You can use a nonslip pad, too, which looks like a giant sponge and helps keeps baby from slipping. Another option is a big dishpan.

Baby carrier

A Snugli® or sling or backpack can be a handy way to carry baby. Not all babies like these, so try them out before you get one, if you can.

Swing

A windup or battery powered ride that keeps baby in motion. Some babies like the rocking motion and some don't. Let baby try before you buy. Also check for age requirements. Some are only safe for older babies.

Baby/infant seat

A reclining seat, with safety straps, lets baby sit up and look around before she can hold her head up.

Playpen

A safe, temporary place for baby to play when you are busy in the same room. Some playpens have soft mesh sides; be careful that they are sturdy and not loose enough for baby to roll into them and get stuck.

(continued)

Baby Stuff: Equipment *(continued)*

You can contact the U.S. Consumer Product Safety Commission at their toll-free hotline at 1-800-638-2772 for safety recall information on cribs, baby bath tubs, highchairs, toys and more.

Buying or borrowing secondhand equipment

Most parents borrow some baby equipment or buy it secondhand. It's a great way to save money, but be sure any used equipment is safe.

All equipment and furniture

- Ask the age of the item. Make sure it meets safety standards. Check for the seal of the Juvenile Products Manufacturing Association (JMPA) for assurance that it meets safety standards.
- Check for missing hardware, loose threads, strings, holes, tears, or other defects.
- Get the original instructions for the item.

Highchair

- Has safety straps between the legs and around the waist.
- Wide stable base.
- Has locking devices to keep it from collapsing.

Crib

- Should be made after 1974 when safety standards were established.
- Meets safety requirements (see Bed on page 26).
- No lead paint.

Car Seat

- Must be newer than 1981 to meet safety standards. Car seats must be labeled and dated, so check.
- Must never have been involved in a crash.
- Has all the parts and instructions for installation.
- Has not been recalled. (Call The National Highway Traffic Safety Administration at 1-800-424-9393 or 1-888-327-4236 (also toll-free) with manufacturer name and model number.)

Security gates

- Avoid old-style accordion folding gates; they pinch fingers, heads, arms.

Playpen

- Mesh must have less than 1/4" openings.
- Mesh must be free of holes or tears and fastened securely to top and bottom.
- Wooden slats must be no more than 2-3/8" apart.

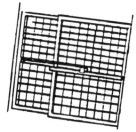

Baby Stuff: Clothes and Supplies

Babies seem to need a lot of clothing and supplies. There are supplies for changing, bathing and feeding which are helpful and handy to have for the first few months. Babies need clothes, too. You can buy some clothes before baby is born, but stick to the basics. How much you get may also be affected by your laundry washing situation. Here are some basics that baby will need for the first few months.

Basic Supplies for the First Months

Clothing
Disposable diapers*	70 (for 1 week)
(Infants use 7 to 10 diapers per day)	840 (for 3 months)
Undershirts	8 total
Sleepers/night shirt	6
Tops	3
Bottoms	4
Blanket sleeper (depending on season)	2
Socks or booties	3 pair
Hat	1
Warm outdoor clothing, if necessary	1 set

Changing Supplies
Prepackaged wipes	3 boxes
Washcloths	2 to 3
Diaper pail/container with tight fitting lid	1

Bed Needs
Crib bumpers	1 set
Crib sheets	3 to 4
Waterproof pads	3 to 4
Blankets Lightweight (receiving blanket)	3 to 4
Warm	2

*If using cloth diapers, you will need safety pins, plastic pants (about 4 to 6) and diapers (about 5 dozen).

Bathtime
Bathtub/dishpan	1
Soft bath towels	3 to 4
Washcloths	3 to 4
Baby soap	1
Baby shampoo	1
Sterile cotton balls	1 bag

Mealtime
If bottle-feeding:
4 oz. bottles	4
8 oz. bottles	6 to 8
Nipples	12
Formula	1 case

If breastfeeding:
Breast pump (optional)	1
4 oz. bottles	2
8 oz. bottles	2
Nipples	4
Formula	2 cans

Bottle brush	1
Bibs	2 to 3
Burp cloths	2 to 3

Health Care
Non-aspirin pain/fever medication recommended by your doctor

Thermometer

Rubbing alcohol, cottonballs

Diaper rash ointment

Playthings
Simple toys are best:
Hanging mobile
Soft, squeaky, chewable rubber toys
Baby-safe, plastic mirror

Budgeting for Baby

Buying all the clothing, supplies and equipment baby needs can be expensive. Planning what you will buy, comparing prices, borrowing, looking into secondhand things, and considering some low cost options, such as using things you have on hand instead of buying new, can all help you save money. Use this form to think about what your baby will need, then do some planning to come up with a reasonable budget for you.

Supplies for the First Few Months

What's Needed	Cost	Options*

*See page 28 for safety tips.

Decisions to Make Before Baby Is Born

Getting ready for baby involves a lot of decision-making. It helps to think the decisions through and talk about them with others who can help. It's a good idea to make the decisions before you go to the hospital. Once labor has started and immediately after baby is born are not the best times to make big decisions.

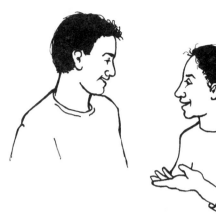

Your child birth class may have given you a Birth Plan form so you can write down the decisions you've made about the birth. These may include who will be in the delivery room with you, whether or not mom may want pain medication, circumcision decision, and more. Be sure to take the plan with you and give it to the nurses who will be with you.

Baby's Name

Names can be exotic or plain, common or unusual; it's a personal choice, but keep in mind that the name you choose is often the first thing people know about baby and they may make some assumptions based on that.

Many cultures think it an honor to have a child named after a living or deceased relative; just as many think it shouldn't be done. Find out what your family thinks.

Unique names and spellings are fine. Just be prepared for misspelled mail and spending time spelling it for everyone you meet.

Names from specific cultures and backgrounds can be wonderful ways to build pride for babies' heritage.

Parents need to discuss which last name baby will have and what goes on the birth certificate.

What about Junior? Many families find this a great source of pride. It can also be confusing if Junior is not added to all your child's formal documents.

If parents can't agree on a name, consider having one choose the first name and the other the middle.

Say the names you like out loud, with the middle and last names. How does it sound?

Picking a name is very personal. Take your time when deciding.

Circumcision Decision

Circumcision, the surgical removal of the foreskin of the penis, used to be routinely done to almost all boy babies in the US. Now, parents want to decide. Because circumcision is done soon after delivery, be prepared with your choice before you go to the hospital. In the delivery room, you will be too involved to look at the pros and cons of the operation. It's recommended that parents make the decision with their doctor and fully consider benefits and risks, including any cultural, social or religious factors.

Getting to the Hospital

Plan how you will get to the hospital. If you're getting a ride, be sure to ask that the car be kept ready to go with gas, etc. As the day gets closer, ask your driver to let you know where she can be reached. If going by taxi, keep the number handy and have cash on hand for the fare. Know who you can call in an emergency or if your plans fall through.

(continued)

Decisions to Make Before Baby Is Born *(continued)*

Pack Your Bags

In general

Pack your bag ahead of time so you are ready to go at a moment's notice!

- Health insurance information.
- Books, portable stereo with music that relaxes you, magazines—labor may last awhile. Take what helps you pass time comfortably.
- Items recommended at child birth class. These could be a tennis ball for massage, snacks for the coach, picture for mom to focus on during labor.
- Phone numbers of people to call. Money for phone calls.
- Camera and film.

Baby's bag

- Two nightshirts that open from the bottom
- Diapers
- Going-home outfit
- Blanket
- Baby hat
- Warm outdoor clothes, if necessary.

Don't forget a car safety seat. Baby is just not safe without it. Also, the hospital may not let baby leave unless you have an approved car seat with you.

Mom's bag

(For ideas for dad's bag, see page 33.)

- Nightgown and robe — front opening for breastfeeding.
- Slippers/socks

- Underclothes — include a nursing bra if needed.
- Personal items — toothbrush, toothpaste, hair care, deodorant, etc. Include maxi-pads, too, for after the birth.
- Comfortable, loose-fitting clothes to go home in.

Paperwork

Even newborn babies are surrounded by paperwork. Call ahead and ask what information you will need. Be prepared with information for these documents:

- Health insurance for the newborn. (Once baby is born she may need different insurance coverage than before she was born.) Bring insurance company name, address, phone number and policy number.
- Information for birth certificate or declaration of paternity. This varies by state, so call your hospital to find out what is needed.
- You will need to apply for a Social Security number for your baby. Some hospitals have the forms right there for you to complete and mail.

Dad's Plan

Dad needs to be ready for baby's birth, too. There are decisions to make and discussions to have with baby's mom about baby's name, insurance, the role you will play in the birth, and many other things. Taking time to do all this may help make the experience of becoming a parent go more smoothly.

Things for Dad to think about:

With baby's mom, work out your role for baby's birth (prenatal classes, labor coach, photographer and more).

_____
_____
_____
_____
_____

How will you find out when baby is about to be born? How will you get to the hospital?

_____
_____
_____
_____

Pack a small bag with things like a clean shirt, toothbrush, shaving supplies, etc., in case the birth takes long time and you need to clean up.

Pack some stuff to pass the time if this turns into a long wait—something to read, a portable stereo (with headphones), music both parents like, money for phones, snacks, etc.

Arrange to have a camera and film for pictures of the baby. Talk with the mom about when and what photos to take.

_____
_____
_____

Include a list of phone numbers for those you want to let know that you're now a dad.

Understand that baby might look a little puffy and squished out of shape because of what he's been through. Be prepared and plan to fall in love with him anyway. What are some things you will do right away to bond with your child?

_____
_____
_____

Understand that your baby's mom might look a little rough because of what she's been through. Be prepared and plan for ways to make her feel respected and honored. How will you do this?

_____
_____
_____

Be prepared to fill out and sign the birth certificate and paternity form. Right there, right then. What will you need to bring with you to do this?

_____
_____
_____

Other:

_____
_____
_____

Plan Ahead for Birth Control

It may seem odd to talk about birth control right before your baby is born. However, now is the time to make some decisions about the birth control methods you will use after the baby is here. Discuss this with your doctor so you will know when mom can resume sexual relations and how to prevent another pregnancy before you're ready.

Keep in mind that the younger a woman is, the sooner she's likely to ovulate after giving birth—even if she's breastfeeding. Ovulation is the time when pregnancy can happen.

Before you choose the method you will use, you need to know yourself and your partner and the situations when you're likely to have sex. These will affect the method you choose. Some methods require preparation and a cooperative partner, while others are more under your control. Ask your doctor or family planning clinic for more information.

Know Yourself

- Are you very careful about taking medicine according to the directions or do you just take it whenever you think of it?

- Do you like routines or does spontaneity appeal to you?

- Are you assertive, able to say what you want and need in a strong, positive way? Are you more passive, likely to just go along with whatever happens, no matter how you feel?

- Do you know when you are likely to have sex or is timing more random?

- How do you regard sex? Is it something that "just happens" or do you think about when, where and why it will take place?

- Some feel they aren't supposed to plan for sex or know that much about their own bodies. What do you think?

- Do you recognize the responsibility for having safe sex both for prevention of pregnancy and to protect yourself from sexually transmitted diseases (STDs)?

- Do you have more than one sex partner?

Know Your Partner

- Is your partner someone you know well and trust? Is this a long-term relationship?

- Does he or she have more than one sex partner?

- Does your partner recognize the responsibility of having safe sex—both as a prevention of STDs and for prevention of pregnancy?

- Some think that sex should just happen whenever it seems "right" without waiting or using any protection. What does your partner think?

- Is your partner comfortable talking about sex?

Know the Situation

- When are you likely to have sex?

- Are you able to keep your birth control method with you at all times when you might have sex?

- Where are you likely to have sex? At home, at your partner's home, somewhere else?

- Is your method easy to use in all situations?

34

Birth Control Methods and How They Work

There are a variety of birth control methods available to women. For men, the condom is the most common method used. You can read over these brief descriptions so you have some idea of what's available and how each is used. Your doctor or a family planning clinic can give you much more information. They will help you decide what would work best for you.

These methods do not prevent pregnancy and should not be used as birth control:

- Having sex during woman's menstrual period or while breastfeeding.
- Using a plastic kitchen wrap as a condom.
- Sitting or standing up during sex.
- Taking a shower afterwards.
- Feminine hygiene products.
- Withdrawal (male withdraws penis from vagina before he "comes.") This method does not prevent pregnancy because:
  - Male might not withdraw.
  - Some sperm arrives before ejaculation.

Condom with spermicide

A man uses a condom which catches sperm, preventing it from reaching the woman's uterus. The woman uses spermicide to kill any sperm not captured by the condom.

Birth control pills

Stops body from releasing ripened egg. "The Pill" is available only by prescription. Doctor will give woman a physical exam and then prescribe.

Female condom with spermicide

Prevents pregnancy the same way a condom does, by acting as a barrier between the sperm and egg. Use with a spermicide.

Diaphragm with spermicide

Must always be used with spermicide to be effective. Prevents sperm from entering uterus. Woman gets fitted by doctor or family planning clinic. Need to practice inserting it under supervision.

Norplant™

Stops ovaries from releasing an egg each month. After a medical exam, the doctor or nurse puts tiny capsules of artificial hormones under skin of arm. Not recommended for breastfeeding women.

Natural birth control

(Also called natural family planning or the rhythm method.)

The woman does not have sexual intercourse at the time of month she releases an egg. **Check with your doctor regarding this method. It takes training and supervision at first.** The woman must figure out when ovulation occurs by calendar, mucus and/or temperature method and she must keep daily records. Intercourse is avoided during "unsafe" times of the month.

Fertility awareness method

Use of a condom or diaphragm with spermicide **only** during the time when pregnancy is most likely which is when the woman's body releases an egg. Body signs are looked for and charted—such as body temperature, vaginal mucus, periods.

Sterilization

An operation that makes a person unable to have a baby. For a man it's called a vasectomy, for a woman it's called a tubal ligation. Check with your doctor regarding this method. It's permanent.

Sex without intercourse

Partners find ways of holding, touching or caressing to give each other sexual pleasure without putting penis in or near vagina.

Abstinence

Choosing not to have sex at all. Pregnancy is impossible when sperm and egg don't meet.

If you think your birth control is making you sick, go see your doctor to talk about a new form of birth control.

© Meld 1999 • 612-332-7563

Your Notes

You can use this page to make notes about things you've learned, questions you have, milestones reached, and more. It can be a record of some of the events in your life as a new parent—your dreams, memories, concerns, hopes, and plans. Or perhaps this is a place to write down and celebrate baby's changes, growth and development —that first tooth, first word, first step...

Chapter 3
At Home With Your Newborn

Bringing baby home is exciting, but it can be scary, too. In the hospital there were people right there to answer your questions and help you, but now it's all up to you! This chapter offers suggestions to help you understand and continue to fall in love with your newborn. It also includes baby care basics—feeding, diapering, comforting and more. There is information about your newborn's growth and learning that includes encouraging ways parents can play with baby.

Mom's Body After Baby's Birth

Delivering a baby is hard work. Mom's body will react to this "labor" in many different ways. She may feel sore and tired. She will experience other physical signs, too. Here are some of the more common changes after delivery. If there are severe symptoms or you're worried, call your doctor.

Vaginal discharge

For three to six weeks mom will have some bleeding. At first it will be bright red, eventually turning a yellowish-white. It can last six weeks.

What to do:
Wear sanitary napkins. Do not use tampons.

Menstruation

Menstrual periods begin again six to 12 weeks after delivery or when mom stops nursing.

Breasts

Mom's breasts will be larger than before, as they fill with milk to feed baby. If breastfeeding, breasts will be larger until after nursing stops. Expect some soreness when milk first comes in. If bottle-feeding, expect breasts to return to normal size in a month or two. There may be engorgement until milk dries up. Breast engorgement can happen when milk comes in (day 3 or 4 after delivery). It can be very uncomfortable and can make it difficult for baby to nurse.

What to do:
Warm cloths applied to breasts, warm baths, or a mild pain killer recommended by your doctor may help. Talk to your doctor if you are having difficulty.

Bottom soreness

If mom had stitches after delivery, there may be discomfort. Hemorrhoids, which may itch, burn, or even bleed, are common after delivery.

What to do:
Try a warm bath a few times a day. If pain persists, call your doctor.

Urination/bowel movements

It's common for mothers to urinate very often and to perspire heavily in the days following delivery. This happens as the body gets rids of the extra fluids from the pregnancy.

It can take time for typical bowel function to return after delivery. To get things back to normal more quickly, eat more fiber, drink more liquids and exercise. Start by taking a short walk at the hospital.

What to do:
Replace lost fluids, especially if breastfeeding, by drinking more water, milk and juice.

Don't let up on eating fruits, vegetables or grains.

Fatigue

Parents feel tired for awhile because childbirth takes a great deal of energy and because it's a very emotional time. You may not get all of the sleep you need because of baby's schedule.

What to do:
Sleep when baby sleeps. Plan to take it easy until you feel more energetic. Ask for and accept help.

Sex

Follow your doctor's advice on when to resume sexual relations. Many say between three to six weeks after delivery. **Remember, mom can become pregnant again even without getting a period or when breastfeeding.** Decide on a birth control method before baby is born.

Baby Blues: Postpartum Depression

Even if mom's body returns to normal very quickly, she may be on an emotional roller coaster after baby is born. She may feel weepy, unhappy, anxious, worried in turn or all at once.

Dad's can experience the blues, too, as he adjusts to his new role, responsibilities and the change in his relationship with baby's mom.

What Is It?

The baby blues, postpartum depression, are probably related to the big change in mom's hormones after delivery, but there are "nonhormonal" causes, too. The blues usually go away within a few days, although some parents find they come and go over the first month or so. Remember, dad can have the "baby blues," too, and may need support just as much as mom.

Some nonhormonal causes:

All eyes on baby

Parents may feel left out now that baby is the center of attention. For nine months, parents, especially mom, were fussed over, but now baby is the star.

Going home

This can be overwhelming, especially if you have no help. A new baby to care for, in addition to your usual responsibilities, may just seem too much to handle.

Disappointment

You may be disappointed in your baby; she's not the cute cuddly baby you expected. Or you may be disappointed at how you reacted during the birth. Or you may be depressed about parenthood; it's just not what you expected.

Exhaustion

Tiredness following delivery, plus the demands of caring for a newborn, can make parents feel they just can't do what's expected.

Missing the old you

Your old lifestyle is gone and you have new responsibilities. Other's expectations of you may be different, too. They may expect you to act like a "parent" now. This can be depressing.

Lack of support

If you don't have anyone to support you, either helping with baby care, listening to your worries and concerns, or just being there for you, you can feel overwhelmed and alone.

Other stress

Worries about money, school, jobs or family can add to depression.

What to Do

There's no sure cure for the baby blues, other than time, but you may be able to ease some of the feelings:

- Limit visitors if they stress you or invite more if they cheer you up.
- Get as much sleep as possible. Sleep when baby sleeps.
- Ask for help from others.
- Eat healthy foods.
- Talk about how you are feeling.
- Get out of the house. Meet a friend or take a walk with baby.
- Be active. Exercise makes a difference.
- Make time for yourself. Doing something just for you can help you feel better.
- Meet other new parents. Talking to those in the same situation helps you realize that you're not alone and the feelings you have are common.
- If the "blues" seem overwhelming or last too long, call your doctor for help.

Taking Care of You

It takes a lot of time and energy to take care of a newborn. Parents need to be sure they have the energy by taking care of themselves. Taking care means maintaining your health and getting the rest you need, and keeping stress at a minimum. Do all you can to be there for baby.

Eat nutritious food
Eat wisely. Junk food and too much sugar can make you feel exhausted and less able to cope. Snack on protein (milk, cheese, tuna). These foods stick with you and help you cope.

Get plenty of rest
If you've had a rough night, take a nap when baby goes down for a nap. If you missed out on a night's sleep, call somebody to watch baby while you rest. When you're tired, your emotions can get the best of you. Don't get so run down that you can't handle taking care of baby.

Exercise
Exercise gets your blood moving through your body. Take a long, fast-paced walk with your baby. You'll be better able to take care of baby when you feel strong and healthy.

Laugh
Laughter is good medicine for just about everything. Learn to laugh at your mistakes, at the funny things baby does, and the world in general. Laughter is a great stress reliever.

Keep things simple
Make your life easier by keeping necessary supplies handy, dressing baby in easy to remove clothes and making simple meals. In the early days, you will have more energy and time if you keep things as simple as possible.

Get out
Feeling cooped up with a baby can rob you of energy and interest in baby's care. Meet a friend, arrange for someone you trust to care for baby, and take some time for you.

Don't worry about the small stuff
Focus on what is important, which right now is getting to know and taking care of baby. Let less important things take second priority for now.

Limit alcohol, medication and drugs
Certain chemicals and substances rob you of your ability to cope effectively with stressful situations. Set limits for yourself so you're always ready to safely and responsibly handle your baby's needs. Breastfeeding mothers should not use alcohol or drugs and should check with their doctor about taking medications.

Expect the unexpected
Life with baby is full of surprises. Just when you're ready to head out the door with baby all bundled up, you hear (or smell!) the need for a diaper change. Build in extra time to handle these little surprises. It can reduce stress.

40

Stuck On You: Bonding and Attachment

You've seen ads that say how tightly a glue will "bond." That means how tight it will stick things together. There can be no tighter bond than that between parents and child. When you are stuck on your baby, she knows how much you love her and that you will take care of her every need. This is important. This bonding or attachment between parent and child gives baby a sense of inner security. A child secure in her parents' love is able to explore the world around her, is ready to learn, and is on the way to a good life. This bond starts even before baby is born and develops after birth during the countless hours parents spend playing with and responding to baby's needs.

Strengthening the Bond

Respond to cries

By going to baby when she cries, you're showing her you are concerned and that you want to take care of her. This builds trust between you. You cannot spoil baby by picking her up or comforting her when she cries, but you can make her feel she's not important by ignoring her. When you respond to cries and other signals, you are showing her that language and communication have a purpose, too.

Take your time

Baby will feel stressed and unsettled if you rush through feeding, changing, bathing and other care. Your baby needs to know that you enjoy your time with him and that his care is your priority.

Babies can do no wrong

Babies don't know the difference between right and wrong—and won't, for several years. Do not punish your young baby. Be loving and patient when baby is doing something you wish she wouldn't—crying, not sleeping—by taking care of her and comforting her.

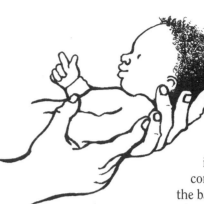

Talking to baby

Even when baby doesn't understand words, he will begin to understand your tone and facial expressions. This first step in communication is fascinating to baby and help build attachment.

Use baby's name

Talk to baby and describe her world. "This is Akila's teddy bear! Akila loves her bear and I love Akila!" This helps her understand she is a separate person from you.

Play with baby in many different ways

Use toys, sing and talk. Show him his fingers and toes and much more. Play is a way to show baby how much you enjoy being with him.

Dads and Bonding

Babies need dads to be attached to them, too, but sometimes there are barriers.

In the beginning, mom and others may assume dad isn't going to be comfortable around the baby or know how to take care of him. They may try to take baby back after letting you hold him for just a quick minute. You can help by speaking up for yourself, by showing that you care deeply about baby, that you know baby care basics and are committed to learning more.

You may not feel for baby all you expected to feel at first. That's OK. The bonding experience isn't immediate and earth-shaking for everybody. Stay close to baby—hold her, feed her, make eye contact, tell her how much you love her. Be patient and give bonding a little time.

Baby's mom may be angry at you because of old problems or because she feels she's carrying this new responsibility all by herself. Be determined to prove over time by your actions that you are serious about being a father to your child.

What Newborns Can Do

Newborn babies are amazing. All their senses are working at birth and they are born with reflexes that keep them alive. Babies can tell parents what they like and don't like, when they are hungry, when they are happy, and many more things about themselves. Watch your newborn and you will learn a lot about him!

Be sure to review the **Keeping Baby Safe** chapter. Babies can often do more than you think and they change quickly, making safety an important part of child care.

All five of baby's senses are working at birth

- Sight. Newborns see things that are about eight inches away the best. She will like looking at bold colors and patterns.
- Hearing. A newborn startles at sudden noises and may cry when he hears other newborns crying. Crying can be soothed by sounds—a lullaby, a heartbeat or a ticking clock.
- Taste. Baby will prefer certain flavors, like formula or breast milk, but not others that are sour or bitter.
- Smell. A newborn turns his head away from strong, unpleasant smells.
- Touch. Baby loves to be touched. Newborns calm to the warmth of your body. Baby will turn toward you if you touch a cheek and will tremble a little when the doctor puts a cold instrument on her chest.

Your newborn is born with reflexes that keep her alive

- Baby can breathe, suck and swallow.
- Her body gets rid of wastes. You will need to change diapers seven to ten times a day!
- She will sleep when there's too much noise around her.

Baby will let you know what he likes and doesn't like

- He will watch human faces more than objects or pictures. He spends more time looking at faces.
- Babies like to have eye contact with parents. Baby will eat better if he can see you watching him.
- How baby reacts to what he sees, hears and smells will tell you what he likes and doesn't like.

Your newborn gives clues about how to care for him

- He cries when hungry, too warm, wet, too excited, lonely or surprised.
- She coos when peaceful and content.
- Baby moves his body—even his toes—to show pleasure.
- She uses her face. She smiles, frowns, shows excitement and frustration.
- Baby turns his head toward your voice or a bottle.
- She turns away from food when full.

Every baby is unique at birth. No two are alike. Each one is special and different in ways like these:

- Her sleep patterns.
- How much she moves around.
- The way and how often he cries.
- Her reactions to sound and light.
- The way he responds to smells.

Getting to Know Your Baby

Spend time getting to know baby by playing with her. A lot of your play will come naturally—you know how to coo, make funny faces, rub noses, and more. About all you need is your face, your touch, the sound of your voice and the gentleness that's exchanged between you during feeding, diapering, bathing and rocking. And while you're having fun doing all that cooing and grinning at baby, you're stimulating his brain to develop and making him feel loved and important.

Touching & Feeling

Gently move baby's arms and legs. Touch her hand, fingers feet and toes. Loving touch helps your baby become aware of her body, to learn what is a part of her and what is not.

Cuddle, hug, kiss and gently caress your baby.

Lay baby on her back, then move arms above her head or push her legs up to bend knees.

While baby's on his stomach, gently push against baby's feet with your hands.

Always touch baby gently. Don't toss her in the air or play rough in other ways.

Seeing

Make faces—smile, frown, laugh, wrinkle up, wink, wiggle your eyebrows and whatever else you can think of. Be silly.

Hang boldly colored and patterned toys, pictures or other things where baby can watch them. Occasionally put a patterned sheet on baby's bed.

Catch baby's attention with something bright. Slowly move the object as baby watches it.

Make a toy disappear and reappear. Act surprised when toy pops up again.

Play peek-a-boo. Move baby's hands in front of his face and then pull hands apart.

Put baby in places where he can see things that move—shadows, sunlight patterns, mobiles, curtains moving in a breeze.

Hearing

Give baby your total attention and talk to him in a friendly voice. Talk about what you're doing or just make playful sounds.

Play a radio in baby's room sometimes.

Talk to baby from different places in the room so baby can begin to coordinate sound and sight.

Make noises—whisper, giggle, whistle, sing, hum and talk, talk, talk.

Read picture books with simple words and bright pictures. Yes, even to your very young baby!

Respond to baby's conversation—take turns "talking." Imitate noises baby makes.

More Ideas

- Babies who are cared for by warm, kind people and have opportunities to touch and explore can be trusted to learn.
- Respond to crying: you're teaching baby she's valuable, that the world can be trusted and that language (crying) has a purpose.
- Change baby's crib location occasionally.
- Place baby nearby for family meals and gatherings. Being around people is natural stimulation.
- Most of all, relax and enjoy your baby. Your baby will benefit if you are having fun, too. Keep in mind, baby loves you and thinks you're the most wonderful, stimulating person in the world.

Baby Basics: Caring for Your Infant

Bathing, feeding, diapering and just holding your baby are the most important things you do in the first few month's of baby's life. This is the best time for the two of you to get to know each other. While you're diapering or drying a just-washed tiny head, talk to your baby. Sing songs. Imitate your baby's sounds. Learn your baby's signals. All the things you do to care for baby increases your love and attachment to baby.

Sponge Bath Daily, until umbilical cord falls off	• Gently wipe baby with warm, damp cloth. Use mild soap. • Rinse off and pat dry. • Use rubbing alcohol on umbilical cord. Dab with cottonball.
Bathing in Tub Usually 2 to 3 times a week	• Find a time when you won't be interrupted. • Choose a warm, safe place. • Use a mild soap, a soft cloth and warm (not hot) water. • Gently wash the top of baby's head to prevent "cradle cap." It's OK to touch the soft spot (fontanelle) on the top. • Newborn skin is often red and scaly. It will clear up. • Wash behind and in the folds of baby's ears. • Don't forget to wash baby's bottom. • If baby is upset, wrap him in a towel and leave it on baby during bath. Being wrapped comforts some babies. • After bath, gently dab a little Vaseline® on penis if circumcision is slightly irritated.

Ears, Eyes and Nails	• Ears clean themselves. Be sure to wash behind baby's ears. If you're concerned, ask your doctor to check baby's ears at the next visit. • To clean baby's eyes use a cottonball and warm water (no soap or oil). Gently wipe the cottonball over one eye, starting in the corner by the nose and working out to the side. • Trim baby's nails when she's asleep. Use regular manicure scissors, baby scissors with rounded ends or small nail clippers. Nails grow rapidly, so you may have to do this once a week.

(continued)

Never leave baby alone in or near water. He could drown. If the doorbell or phone rings, ignore it or wrap baby in a towel and take him with you.

Don't use cotton swabs or any other objects to clean your baby's ears. You only push the natural protective wax farther into the ear.

Don't leave baby alone even for a second on the changing table. She could quickly flip or roll right off. Use straps and keep one hand on her at all times.

Diapering 7 to 10 times a day	• Keeping bottom dry and clean helps prevent diaper rash. • Clean diaper area with warm water, soap, then rinse bottom. Pat dry. Or, if you use prepackaged wipes, use nonalcohol, hypo-allergenic wipes. Always wipe from front to back. • Do not use baby powder or special lotions. They may irritate skin. • If you wash cloth diapers, use Ivory Snow® or Dreft®. Rinse an extra time and add one cup white vinegar to last rinse.	
Diaper Rash When it occurs	• Do all of the above when diapering. • Leave diapers off baby 10 to 15 minutes, three to four times a day to give baby's bottom more time to dry. • Ask your doctor to recommend a diaper rash ointment. There are many, but one commonly used is A&D® ointment. Zinc oxide ointment is also good, but don't overuse. It can cause a burn.	
Feeding— **by any method** Every 2-1/2 to three or four hours, depending on baby's schedule	• **Sit down, relax and take your time.** • **Always hold baby.** • **Get to know your baby's signals:** – Baby will let you know he is hungry by chewing fingers, with a tearless, hungry cry or a slightly opened mouth. – Baby will show you she is ready to eat by turning her head, by opening mouth, sucking, clenching fists and making contact with your chest. – As baby feels full, she will let you know by unfolding fingers, turning head away, falling asleep or showing you a brighter, cheerier face. Learn your baby's signals of hunger and when he's full. Responding to these signals shows him you understand and care about his needs. • **Remember, babies have growth spurts.** That means they grow a lot at three weeks, six weeks and three months. Babies who are fussy at those ages may need to eat more.	

(continued)

Call your doctor if:

• Baby needs to be fed every hour.
• Your newborn is crying so much you cannot cope.
• Baby is vomiting often (some spitting up is normal).
• Your baby is not gaining weight or eating enough. You can see this if it happens; baby's face isn't getting rounder or if baby doesn't need 7 to 10 diaper changes a day. If baby isn't eating enough in the first two or three weeks of life, call for a doctor's appointment.

Feeding— by any method *(continued)*	If mom is breastfeeding, she will need to drink more milk, juice or water at those times and nurse baby more often until her supply increases. This usually happens in two or three days.
	• **Do not give baby any solid foods until she is about six months old.** Babies can't digest solids until then. They won't get the right balance of calories if they are given solids rather than all breast milk or formula. Check with your doctor if you have questions.
Breastfeeding Depends on baby's schedule. Every 2-1/2 to three or four hours 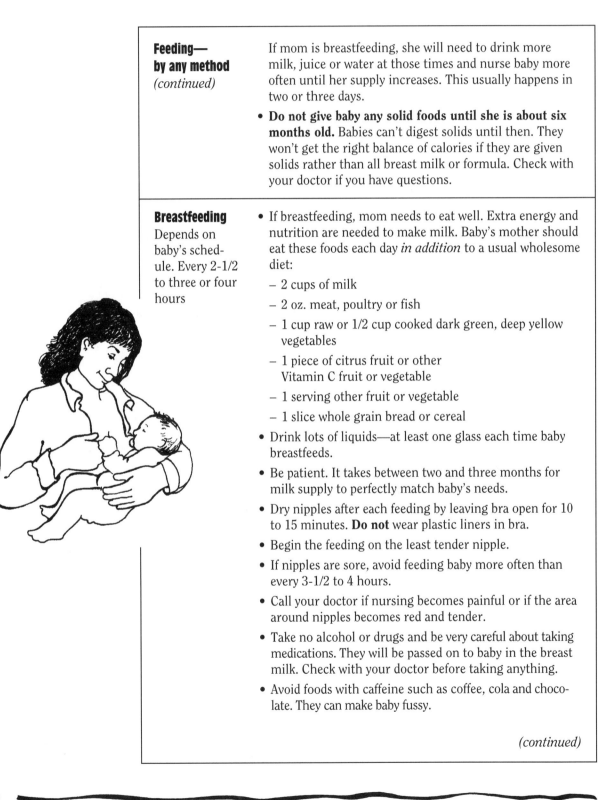	• If breastfeeding, mom needs to eat well. Extra energy and nutrition are needed to make milk. Baby's mother should eat these foods each day *in addition* to a usual wholesome diet:
	– 2 cups of milk
	– 2 oz. meat, poultry or fish
	– 1 cup raw or 1/2 cup cooked dark green, deep yellow vegetables
	– 1 piece of citrus fruit or other Vitamin C fruit or vegetable
	– 1 serving other fruit or vegetable
	– 1 slice whole grain bread or cereal
	• Drink lots of liquids—at least one glass each time baby breastfeeds.
	• Be patient. It takes between two and three months for milk supply to perfectly match baby's needs.
	• Dry nipples after each feeding by leaving bra open for 10 to 15 minutes. **Do not** wear plastic liners in bra.
	• Begin the feeding on the least tender nipple.
	• If nipples are sore, avoid feeding baby more often than every 3-1/2 to 4 hours.
	• Call your doctor if nursing becomes painful or if the area around nipples becomes red and tender.
	• Take no alcohol or drugs and be very careful about taking medications. They will be passed on to baby in the breast milk. Check with your doctor before taking anything.
	• Avoid foods with caffeine such as coffee, cola and chocolate. They can make baby fussy.

(continued)

Breastfeeding *(continued)*	• Don't let breastfeeding tie you to the house. Mothers can still go to school or work, with some rearranging. You can and should get out for the evening now and then, too.
	• If worried about mom not having enough milk, look at:
	– Seven or more wet diapers a day is a sign baby's getting enough breast milk.
	– Offer both breasts at each feeding. Let baby empty at least one breast at each feeding.
	– Don't offer too many bottles of formula or water—three to four a week is enough.
	– Some medications interfere with milk production.
	– Being stressed or overtired can interfere with milk production.
Bottle-feeding	• Sit down, relax and enjoy your baby completely when you feed him.
	• How to make baby formula:
	– **Canned concentrate:** Wash off the top of the can, open it with a clean can opener and mix concentrate with tap water as directed.
	– **Powdered formula:** Add water as instructed. Stir while adding powder to the water to avoid lumps.
	– Never add more water than directions call for. Formula with too much water won't have the proper nutrition.
	– Put bottles of formula in the refrigerator right away. If you don't have a refrigerator available, make only one bottle at a time, right before feeding.
	– When finished, rinse bottles with cold water first. Then wash in soapy water. Get milk out of nipple opening by forcing water through the hole. Use a bottle brush. Or use a dishwasher for the bottles.
	– It's not necessary to sterilize bottles and nipples if you follow these directions and are careful about keeping things clean.
	• Each baby will have a preference for warm or cold formula. Try both to see what your baby likes. It's fine to feed baby cold formula right from the refrigerator. If you

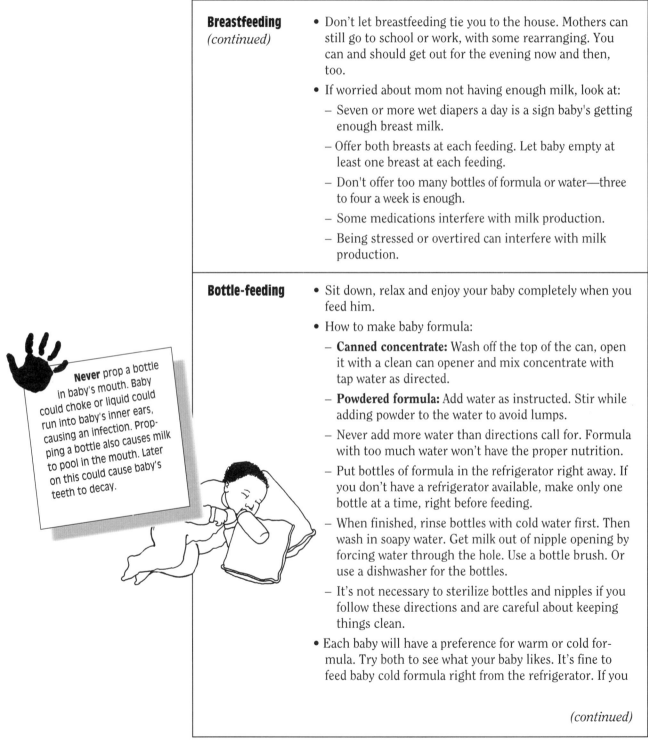

Never prop a bottle in baby's mouth. Baby could choke or liquid could run into baby's inner ears, causing an infection. Propping a bottle also causes milk to pool in the mouth. Later on this could cause baby's teeth to decay.

(continued)

Bottle-feeding *(continued)*	want to warm it, just hold bottle under hot water faucet or heat gently in a pan of water on the stove. DO NOT BOIL. Don't heat in microwave, either. It can heat unevenly and cause burns. Don't warm bottle by just letting it sit out of the refrigerator—formula can spoil that way. • Before giving baby bottle, shake a few drops on your wrist. It should be warm, not hot.
Burping During feeding and when baby is finished eating	• Hold your infant over your shoulder or tummy down on your lap. Pat baby's back gently. Do this at least twice during a feeding—or more often. If baby falls asleep during the feeding and hasn't burped, let him lie down until he wakes up again and then burp. 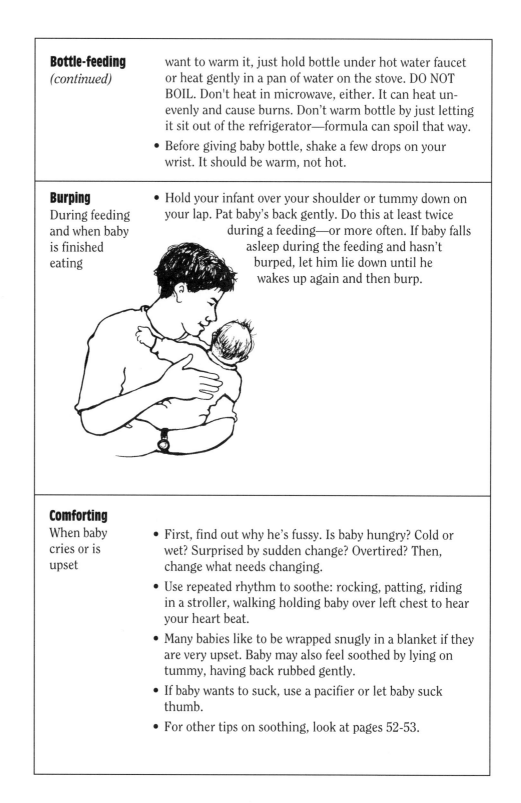
Comforting When baby cries or is upset	• First, find out why he's fussy. Is baby hungry? Cold or wet? Surprised by sudden change? Overtired? Then, change what needs changing. • Use repeated rhythm to soothe: rocking, patting, riding in a stroller, walking holding baby over left chest to hear your heart beat. • Many babies like to be wrapped snugly in a blanket if they are very upset. Baby may also feel soothed by lying on tummy, having back rubbed gently. • If baby wants to suck, use a pacifier or let baby suck thumb. • For other tips on soothing, look at pages 52-53.

On the Go With Baby

You will want to take your baby to visit friends and relatives. Planning and packing can make any outing go more smoothly. Think ahead to what you might need while you're gone—clean diapers, wipes, clean clothes, food for baby—and pack some extra "just in case."

In the Bag

You will need baby supplies and something to carry them in when you and baby are on the go. Smart packing can keep baby and you clean, fed, and comfortable. Remember to replace any supplies you use, so the bag is ready to go.

Diaper bags come in many sizes and shapes. Choose the one which best meets your needs. Or, look around and see what else might work—a backpack, athletic bag or tote bag can be great.

Things to pack:
- Diapers, wipes and diaper ointment
- Changing pad
- Extra clothes
- Plastic bags for wet clothes
- Hat and jacket
- Baby's food, bib
- Baby's special blanket
- Playthings
- Any necessary medicine
- Money for phone or cab
- List of phone numbers and addresses for cab, doctor, work or school and other important numbers
- Important medical and emergency information

Car Seat

Any time a baby rides in any vehicle, she must be in a federally-approved car seat. This is the law in every state, but even more than that, it's the only safe way for a baby to travel. Car seats are not required on city buses or trains.
(See page 26.)

Other Safety Concerns

Visiting grandma or a friend is fun, but you need to be aware of baby's surroundings. Keep alert for possible safety hazards. Childproof the area where baby will be and make sure someone responsible is keeping an eye on baby at all times.

Remember that old cribs may not be safe; check it out before letting baby sleep in one.

When changing baby's diaper, choose a place baby can't roll off of or use the floor.

Check any area where baby plays. Remove small objects and other hazards. Think about open medicine bottles, cigarettes, pets, cleaning supplies, open stairways, dangling electric cords, access to water and more.
(See pages 84-92.)

Good Night, Baby

A bedtime routine can be very comforting to baby. It makes him feel safe and secure if he knows what to expect each evening when he heads to bed. Parents can develop any routine that fits their style, but it's a good idea to have a "portable" routine—one that can be followed no matter where baby is— at home, at grandma's or visiting friends in the evening.

Most parents learn that bedtime isn't the time for tickling and active play. As bedtime approaches, begin to wind things down for baby by playing in quieter ways.

A bedtime routine can include any or all of these ideas and should be matched to both your needs and baby's. Here are ideas for a routine to consider:

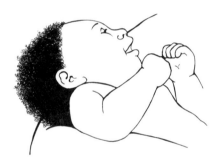

1. Quiet play time

2. Bath
A soothing warm bath can calm baby and get her drowsy and ready for bed.

3. Put on PJs
Cozy PJs with no rough seams or scratchy parts will keep her warm and comfortable.

4. Bedtime feeding
Breast or bottle-fed babies will probably have one last snack before going to sleep. Try to avoid feeding baby to sleep—letting her eat until she is asleep. You want her to be able to fall asleep without needing to eat first.

5. Read to baby
Even the youngest baby can be read to before bed. Babies love the warmth and closeness of being held by you and they are comforted by the rhythmic sound of your voice reading a poem or story.

6. Sing softly
Lullabies are a traditional way to send baby off to dreamland. Even if you can't sing very well, your baby will still love to hear your voice singing whichever song you choose.

7. Tucking in
Dim the lights and tuck baby in as the final step in the routine. Some babies like a special blanket or soft toy as a comforting "lovey" to sleep with. Leave once you're done so he will get used to settling in and going to sleep (even if he cries for you to stay).

But what if baby keeps on crying?

Here is a plan that has worked for many parents: if your child cries when you leave, come back and say "good night" again. Tell her you are close by but it's time to go to sleep, and then leave. Don't turn bright lights on or stay until she sleeps. Some parents reassure with a gentle touch but don't pick her up. If she cries again, wait for a few minutes and then come back and quietly repeat your message. You may need to repeat this many times but after a week or so your child will usually get to sleep on her own.

Remember that all children need help to go to sleep sometimes. You know about these things. You can help your child. Be patient, stay calm and keep in mind that your little baby can't stay awake forever. (See pages 137-140 for more ways to help baby sleep.)

Back Sleeping Safest for Babies
Research shows that young babies who sleep on their stomachs are at greater risk for Sudden Infant Death Syndrome (SIDS) than babies who sleep on their backs. Always position your young baby to sleep on his back. Side sleeping can be a substitute in some cases, but back sleeping is clearly best.

Why Babies Cry

Babies cry for lots of reasons, but the biggest one is to tell parents something isn't right. Babies cry when they are hungry, need a diaper change, are lonely or bored, are hurt, or want to play. Since they don't have words, they must use what they have to communicate, which is crying. Listen to your baby when she cries. You will be able to tell a hungry cry from a bored cry with some practice. When baby cries, always try to comfort and fix what is upsetting her.

Newborns

- Immediately after birth, crying helps fill baby's lungs with air.

- Crying is the way newborns communicate. Without crying, baby might not survive.

- Newborns cry an average of 2-1/2 hours a day. A parent can't always stop newborn crying altogether. Try to understand why the baby is crying so you can soothe her.

- Crying is baby's way to let you know that he needs the security of being held. If he's rocked and walked, it's more like the familiar movement of mom's body before birth.

- Crying tells parents that baby is hungry, wet, tired, too warm or cold, startled, over-stimulated from too much handling or noise, in pain and more.

- Newborns can't tell the difference between you and him. Sometimes he cries when he senses that you are tired or stressed.

3 to 6-Month-Olds

- Some of the same things bother him that did when he was a newborn: hunger, wetness, being overtired, overstimulated, getting bumped and more.

- She's not quite happy. This is kind of a grumbly cry. You may hear it when baby's beginning to be bored or lonely.

- He's angry. Baby will cry to tell you that he doesn't like something or wants you to come back.

- She has a more active temperament. Active babies sleep less and are more frustrated by confining clothing or not having enough to look at or touch. (See pages 113-115.)

6 to 12-Month-Olds

- Your baby will continue to be upset by the basics: hunger, discomfort, fatigue and more.

- Teething is a common cause of crying at this age.

- Baby is afraid more often because he's becoming aware of his world. Vacuum cleaners, clothes pulled over his head, water going down the drain may now be scary. He's afraid of the unexpected—when a stranger comes near or a dog barks. When possible, tell baby ahead of time about what is going to happen next.

- Your little one feels helpless—to get you to understand she wants to be taken with you when you leave the room, helpless to reach a toy that has been dropped. Being able to crawl helps this kind of crying—so does parents' watching for baby's cues.

- Baby may feel frustrated about not being able to open something or make a plaything work. This crying may increase when learning new skills. Some frustration is good for children—it makes them want to learn. Some is unavoidable because what they want to do is unsafe, and they must be stopped from doing unsafe things. Offering baby something else to do can often help her stop crying.

Ways to Soothe a Crying Baby

Remember, when baby cries there is a reason. It's up to you to find the reason and try to solve the problem for baby. Parents quickly learn what baby needs when he cries and how to soothe him. Here are some things to try.

Check the Basics

First, look at and feel your baby.

- Is baby hungry?
- Does baby have a wet diaper or wet clothing?
- Does baby have a tummy ache? (Try burping again or gently patting baby.)
- Is baby's bed dry and comfortable?
- Is baby too warm or too cool?
- Is there something that's hurting baby? (diaper rash, teething, something scratchy, etc.)
- Is baby sick? Does she have a fever?

Next, try:

When you've taken care of all the basics, see if baby can settle himself. Your voice saying quietly, "You can do it," while gently patting his back may help.

If you feel like you may be overstressed, consider joining a parent support group. At meetings, you'll be able to discuss your feelings and experiences while learning techniques that other parents use to get through the tough times.

Other Ideas to Try

Movement

- Try using a rocking chair or automatic baby swing.
- Go for a car ride.
- Carry baby on a tour of the house—look at mirrors and windows.
- Go for a walk outside— try a front carrier, a stroller or your arms.

Baby comfort

- Some babies love to have all their clothes off.
- Others want to be wrapped snugly. Try swaddling baby in a blanket.

- Lay your hand gently on top of baby's head. This comforts some babies.
- If baby is startled by bath water, wrap him in a diaper or soft blanket before getting him wet.
- Some babies are comforted by a special blanket or soft toy to touch and stroke.
- For tummy pain or gas—lay baby across your knees on her stomach and gently rub or pat her back.
- Try placing a **warm** hot water bottle on baby's tummy. (Check the temperature to make sure it's not too hot).

- If baby is fussy when trying to have a bowel movement, let baby push her feet against your hand or body.

Sucking

- Don't use food as a first solution, particularly if baby has just eaten. Adding more food to an already full stomach will add to baby's discomfort.
- Use a pacifier or baby's thumb, if baby seems comforted by sucking. Teach baby to suck her thumb by gently guiding her thumb to her mouth.

(continued)

52

Ways to Soothe a Crying Baby *(continued)*

- If crying seems worse at three weeks, six weeks, or three months, baby may be hungry because he's having a growth spurt. Baby's eating needs change as they grow, and then they do need more to eat.

- If baby is being breast-fed and she's very fussy, you may want to check some of mom's routines (getting enough sleep, change in diet, drinking enough fluids, reducing stress).

Seeing

- Mobile, patterned crib bumper and other things to look at.
- Turn on a night light (or darken room if it's too light).

- Try a baby-safe plastic mirror in the crib for baby to watch herself.

Listening

- Play soft, soothing music.
- Hang wind chimes, musical mobiles.
- Sing, hum and talk to baby.
- Try the noise of a vacuum cleaner (after six months old this might scare baby).

Things I've learned that soothe my baby:

_____

_____

_____

_____

_____

_____

_____

_____

_____

_____

Coping With Colic

A typical newborn spends about 2-1/2 hours a day crying. Your baby will probably cry the most between the ages of two weeks and two months. By the time he is three months old, typical crying times should occur less often and become more predictable.

Colic is another story. Colic is thought to be extreme stomach pain for baby that results in long sessions of crying, often in the early evening. No one really knows what causes colic, nor can it be "cured." Patient parents are the key to helping a colicy baby.

If you think your baby has a problem with crying that isn't colic, see your doctor to make sure baby isn't sick.

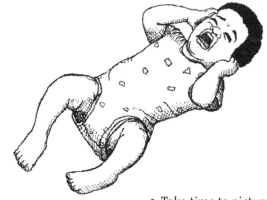

Your Baby Might Have Colic If:

- He cries frantically, draws knees up to his stomach and seems to have a tummy ache.
- Crying stops for a little while, then starts again.
- Crying episodes last three hours or longer.
- Baby can't be comforted by the basics—affection, food, dry diapers, cuddling, etc.

Ways to Help

Colic isn't an "illness" that can be cured, but there are some things you can try to ease a colicy baby's discomfort.

- Don't feed baby unless he is hungry. Sometimes food can cause more problems.
- Do what you can to soothe baby, even though it doesn't seem to be doing any good. Your baby still needs to hear your voice and feel your warmth and affection. Sometimes a walk around the block or a ride in the car will help her.
- Try other soothing measures, such as rubbing baby's tummy, offering him a bottle of warm water, using an automatic baby swing.
- It can be very stressful and scary to deal with this kind of crying all alone. Even being able to take a break by going for a short walk will help. Plan for regularly scheduled breaks from taking care of your colicy baby by lining up babysitters ahead of time. (Be sure babysitter is prepared for a colicy baby and can handle the crying.) Knowing that you will be able to get away soon, will help.
- Ask someone to help you do errands and household chores so you have the time and energy to deal with your crying child.
- Take time to picture your baby as a happy, contented child. Realize your patience and affection during this rough period will help this dream become a reality.
- Keep reminding yourself there is nothing wrong with your baby or with your ability to be a good parent.

Keeping Your Cool With a Crying Baby

A baby crying nonstop from colic or any other reason, can be very stressful and frustrating. After all, a baby's cry is supposed to alert parents to a problem. If you have checked everything there is to check, tried all the soothing techniques, and baby is still crying, you may feel close to losing control. Try these things to cool down.

Never take your anger out on your baby. Don't hit, throw, shove or shake your child. Shaking a baby can cause brain damage or even kill a baby.

Tune Out

Try ear plugs, which will dull the sound but not completely block it out. This can help you get a grip on the situation and your feelings, but you will still be able to hear any changes in the cry. Playing music may also help.

Talk to Yourself

Remind yourself that: the crying won't last forever; you are a good parent; baby loves you and you love your baby; everything will calm down eventually; you can handle this; all babies cry; and more. Keep repeating words that are positive and meaningful to you. Say them out loud or silently. Try whispering, singing, chanting or whatever helps you.

Do Something

You may be able to immediately diffuse your anger or frustration if you pound your fists into a mattress, exercise vigorously, pray, breathe deeply, take a shower, cry or yell to your heart's content. Put baby in a safe place, and then let go!

Call Someone

Pick up the phone and call a family member, friend, parent hotline or emergency service. Or dial 911, and the operator will direct your call to the appropriate person or agency. Let the person know that you want to talk to someone because you feel very stressed and you want to make sure you do nothing that would hurt your child.

Get Someone to Come Over

Sometimes just talking with someone is enough, but if your feelings are overwhelming it might be helpful to have someone come over and help you get through all the anger and stress. There isn't a law against losing your temper, but there is a law against abusing and harming your child. Calling for help is a sign of strength—it shows you care enough about your child and yourself to get help when you need it.

Put Your Child in a Safe Place

If you do feel like things are getting out of control and you might end up doing something violent, carefully put baby in the crib or playpen and go into another room until you calm down and are back in control of yourself. Then immediately call for help.

Your Notes

You can use this page to make notes about things you've learned, questions you have, milestones reached, and more. It can be a record of some of the events in your life as a new parent—your dreams, memories, concerns, hopes, and plans. Or perhaps this is a place to write down and celebrate baby's changes, growth and development —that first tooth, first word, first step...

Chapter 4
Feeding Baby

This chapter is all about feeding babies six months to two years old. If you would like to know about feeding newborns, see Chapter 2: Nine Months Long (page 25) and Chapter 3: At Home With Your Newborn (pages 45-48.)

In the early months, you will spend a lot of time feeding baby. Whether you choose to breast or bottle-feed, you will be responding to baby's hunger signals and making sure he is getting what he needs. As baby grows, his eating will change, too. Get baby off to a good start by understanding his food and nutrition needs, how he will react to foods and recognizing your own responses to food.

Food For Thought

Food can get to be a battleground between parents and children. This can happen when parents look at food as more than a source of nutrition. Parents may use food as a reward or bribe, a sign of love, or a way to measure their parenting. If parents understand these things and look at food as a source of energy and nutrition, a lot of issues over food can be avoided. Here is some food for thought.

Know Your Baby

- A baby determines his own feeding schedule based on what his body tells him. Respond to his hunger cries; don't try to force baby to eat on your schedule.

- Babies can't eat solid foods until they are about six months old. Giving a baby solids before that can interfere with her getting the nutrition she needs. This in turn can make her cranky or hinder her development.

- Baby's need for food changes as he grows. Infants grow rapidly and need many calories. As a toddler's growth slows down, so does his food intake.

- Food is one part of her life that a toddler can control. She may use this control to show her independence by refusing to eat, by insisting on eating **only** cereal, or by drowning her meal in ketchup.

- There are reasons some kids are picky eaters. A child's taste is more concentrated than an adult's. Right now some things really do taste yucky!

- Children do eat less than adults, but may need to eat more often.

- Temperament affects mealtimes. A night owl may not be interested in breakfast as soon as she wakes up. A very focused child may have trouble switching from one thing to another.

- Attention spans are short. Calm, leisurely meals with time for good conversation are probably not yet possible.

- Eye–hand coordination is still developing. Your child's ability to eat neatly will improve as small motor skills develop.

- Do you worry about your little one's eating habits? The child who is growing normally, has a good energy level and is relatively healthy, is getting the food he needs. Talk to your doctor if you are still worried.

Know Yourself

- Think about what food means to you. Many of us regard food as a sign of love and nurturing. When a child refuses food we offer, we can feel rejected. Don't take it personally if a child doesn't want to eat the meal you prepared.

- Was food an issue with you as a child—either you ate too much and were "fat" or ate too little and were "skinny?" Is this affecting how you approach your child and food?

- Know your own eating patterns. Are you a snacker? Do you need to eat on schedule? Children learn from those around them. If you don't eat breakfast, "graze" throughout the day, and then eat a hurried dinner, your child's will soon do these things, too.

- Don't get too worried about a child's eating

(continued)

58

habits. The more you fuss, the greater the chance your child will fuss right back. No one wins a food fight—everyone ends up frustrated.

- Take time to learn some nutrition facts and apply what you know to your meal planning.

- Understanding child development and nutrition needs can help parents have realistic expectations both for behavior at the table and for how much a child needs to eat.

- Respect a child's taste preferences. Chances are you wouldn't serve liver to a friend who hates it, no matter how "good for you" it is. Give your child the same consideration.

Know the Situation

- Young children are creatures of habit. If they are used to eating at a certain time every-day, they will become to depend on food at that time. Getting off schedule for meals can result in problems when you do get around to eating. If you know something is going to change the meal schedules, offer healthy snacks or provide other food to avoid upsets.

- Meals in restaurants or other places away from home can be both fun and challenging. Plan ahead for ways to help your child handle differences in food, expectations, schedules and people.

- No one is at their best when tired and cranky. Plan meals to avoid the worst of times, if possible.

- Food can play a big role in family celebrations. Be prepared to deal with food issues if you and your family have different ideas about food, such as when it's OK to have sweets, or if you choose a different kind of diet from your family's.

What Babies Eat at Different Ages

Babies younger than six months old need to eat only breast milk or formula. Starting at about six months, you can begin feeding baby cereal and gradually add other solid foods.

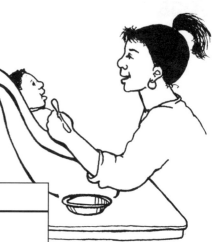

6 to 9 Months Old

Follow this sample menu for two weeks. After that you can add other foods one at a time.

Time	What to Feed Your Baby
Early Morning	Breast milk or 6 to 8 oz. of infant formula.
Mid-Morning	Rice cereal mixed with breast milk or formula. Breast milk or infant formula to drink.
Lunch	Breast milk or 6 to 8 oz. of infant formula.
Dinner	Rice cereal mixed with breast milk or infant formula. Breast milk or infant formula to drink.
Evening or Before Bedtime	Breast milk or 6 to 8 oz. of infant formula. Rice cereal mixture is OK at this time, too.

Remember:
Don't put baby to bed with a bottle. This can lead to ear infections or tooth decay. Plus, feeding time is a good time to cuddle with baby.

More About Feeding

- **Milk** — Breast milk or infant formula is the main food in the diet. Begin use of a cup at meals. Do not give baby cow's milk.

- **Cereal** — Introduce each type of cereal: first rice, then oatmeal, barley or mixed cereal. Feed each for at least two weeks. After that, you can feed baby what she likes. Offer cereal twice a day, with formula or breast milk.

- **Fruits** —can be added after 2 to 3 weeks of cereal only, add one-half jar of any single fruit at the middle of the day. Later offer twice a day. Juice may be substituted for a fruit, but avoid orange and grapefruit juices until baby is over one year old. Baby can't digest them. Watch for allergies.

- **Vegetables** — after 2 to 3 weeks on cereal and fruit, add one-half jar of vegetable to a feeding. Later offer twice a day.

- **Water** — Offer water every day, especially in warm weather.

Hints

- Feed baby using a baby spoon or other small spoon. This helps keep the bites baby-size.

- Give baby only one new food at a time and wait 4 to 5 days before adding any other foods. This way, you'll be able to tell what food causes reactions if baby has a problem.

- Don't feed baby from a jar. Food may become contaminated from germs on spoon. Put a small amount of baby's food in a clean bowl, throw away any un-eaten food.

- Refrigerate unused baby food in the jar for no more than one day.

- Don't feed your baby honey. It contains organisms that can make a baby this age sick.

(continued)

What Babies Eat at Different Ages *(continued)*

9 to 12 Months Old

This is just a sample menu. See More About Feeding for other foods for baby.

Time	What to Feed Your Baby
Early Morning	• 4 tablespoons of infant cereal with breast milk or infant formula • one-half jar of fruit • breast milk or 4 to 8 oz. of formula to drink
Mid-Morning	• 4 oz. of juice • finger foods (see page 64)
Lunch	• one-half jar of fruit (3 oz.) • one-half jar of vegetables (3 oz.) • one-half jar of meat (3 oz.) or protein food • breast milk or 4 to 8 oz. formula
Mid-Afternoon	• 4 oz. of juice • finger foods
Dinner	• 4 tablespoons of infant cereal with breast milk or formula • one-half jar of vegetables or one-half jar of meat (3 oz.) • one-half jar of vegetables (3 oz.) • breast milk or 4 to 8 oz. of formula to drink
Evening or Before Bedtime	• breast milk or 6 to 8 oz. of formula. Cereal and fruit at this time are OK, too.

10 to 12 months. Check with your doctor first.

- **Cereal** — keep feeding baby cereals as long as possible. Then offer one serving of adult cereal, such as Cream of Wheat®, Cheerios® or oatmeal. Many adult cereals contain a lot of sugar, so read labels for sugar content first.
- **Fruits** — cut soft fruit into small pieces. Serve twice a day.
- **Vegetables** — use small pieces of soft, fresh or frozen vegetables. Serve twice a day.
- **Meats** — meat is usually hard to chew, so puree meat or use jars of single meats.

Hints

- Your baby may want to feed himself. Even though this can make a big mess, he needs to learn how to feed himself.
- Your baby may eat best in a highchair. It helps him sit up.
- You can begin to offer juice and water in a cup.

More About Feeding

- Offer foods that allow baby to feed himself. See page __ for a list of good finger foods.
- **Milk** — continue giving breast milk or formula. Let baby use a cup more often.
- **Milk Products** — give your baby small cheese cubes, puddings and yogurt.
- **Water** — offer water every day, especially in warm weather.
- **Juices** — citrus juices may be introduced at

(continued)

12 to 18 Months Old

This is just a sample menu. Children this age will start to tell you what they want to eat.

Time	What to Feed Your Baby
Early Morning	• one-half cup cereal mixed with milk • fruit • one-half cup milk to drink
Mid-Morning	• one-half cup milk or juice • finger foods (see page 64)
Lunch	• one-half cup fruit • one-fourth cup vegetables • 2 oz. of meat or protein food • one-half cup milk or juice • bread or one-half cup cereal
Mid-Afternoon	• one-half cup milk or juice • finger foods
Dinner	• one-fourth cup fruit • one-half cup vegetables • 2 oz. of meat or protein food • one-half cup milk or juice • bread or one-half cup cereal
Evening or Before Bedtime	• one-half cup milk or juice

Hints

- Try to feed your toddler before he gets too hungry or tired.
- It is not important which food is eaten at which time. It's OK if a toddler wants to eat cereal for dinner and meat and vegetables for breakfast.
- Finger foods may be a big part of a your child's diet at this age. Serve healthy finger foods.
- Don't give low-fat or skim milk to your baby. She needs the fats in whole milk.
- It's not healthy to add extra spices, salt, butter, sugar or honey to a toddler's food.
- Toddlers are messy. Putting plastic or newspaper underneath the highchair can make cleanup easier.

Tips for Weaning Baby:

- Middle-of-the-day breastfeedings are easier to cut out first.
- Take three to four days to a week between each eliminated feeding to allow time for your milk supply and your child to adjust.
- Drink less.
- If breasts are uncomfortable, express just enough milk to relieve discomfort. Hot baths or cloths may help.
- Remember to substitute cuddling for nursing.
- Expect to feel some temporary sadness.

More About Feeding

- **Milk** is a main source of calcium. A child who doesn't like milk can get calcium from other foods like: cheese, cottage cheese, yogurt or ice cream. One-year-olds can drink cow's milk. A toddler needs 2-1/2 cups of milk or other calcium food per day.

- **Fruit and vegetables** can be eaten raw or cooked. They can be fresh, frozen or canned.
- **Cereal/bread** — crackers, pancakes, tortillas or pasta can be served in place of bread or cereal.
- **Eggs** can be added after baby is one year old. Serve eggs instead of meat at a meal.

Toddler's Diet

This is what a one to two-year-old typically eats in one day. Toddlers often like to eat many small meals throughout the day. You can mix, match and divide up these recommended quantities across all your child's meals and snacks throughout the day.

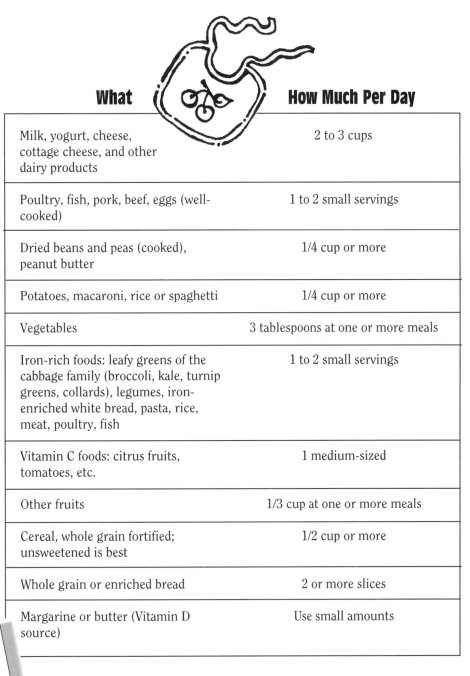

What	How Much Per Day
Milk, yogurt, cheese, cottage cheese, and other dairy products	2 to 3 cups
Poultry, fish, pork, beef, eggs (well-cooked)	1 to 2 small servings
Dried beans and peas (cooked), peanut butter	1/4 cup or more
Potatoes, macaroni, rice or spaghetti	1/4 cup or more
Vegetables	3 tablespoons at one or more meals
Iron-rich foods: leafy greens of the cabbage family (broccoli, kale, turnip greens, collards), legumes, iron-enriched white bread, pasta, rice, meat, poultry, fish	1 to 2 small servings
Vitamin C foods: citrus fruits, tomatoes, etc.	1 medium-sized
Other fruits	1/3 cup at one or more meals
Cereal, whole grain fortified; unsweetened is best	1/2 cup or more
Whole grain or enriched bread	2 or more slices
Margarine or butter (Vitamin D source)	Use small amounts

Families who are vegetarians need to take special care with their child's diet. Talk to your doctor or a nutritionist to be sure you are feeding your child what she needs to grow and stay healthy and strong.

Finger Foods

Baby is usually ready to begin eating finger foods when she is around nine months old. She can use her fingers well enough to pick up small pieces and she is becoming interested in feeding herself.

Not all finger foods are good for babies and toddlers. Some foods can cause choking, others may cause upset stomachs. Still others have no food value—they're called junk foods for good reasons! Since babies and toddlers eat such small quantities, every mouthful must count. Avoid junk foods so babies don't fill up on these non-nutritious foods.

Avoid sweet junk foods!

They easily spoil baby's appetite for nutritious foods and cause tooth decay.

- Soda pop and other sugary drinks or powders mixed with water or milk.
- Candy, cookies, cake, jelly and jam, sugary cereals, pastries, pudding, ice cream, frozen treats, "breakfast "bars.

Why Offer Finger Foods?

Finger foods are good because:

- Your child may eat more food when she feeds herself.
- Baby can practice using his fingers.
- It's a good way for parents to give baby more fresh foods and to introduce new foods.
- Offering finger foods makes feeding baby easier for parents.
- Baby has fun, learns about her world and becomes more independent.

Some good finger foods:

- Mashed bananas or small slices of banana
- Applesauce
- Cooked cereals
- Cheerios® or other similar low-sugar cereal
- Toast, graham crackers, matzos (unsalted), low sodium crackers, soft tortillas, bread sticks, arrowroot biscuits
- Small pieces of soft, fresh, frozen or canned fruits and vegetables (cook, chop and/or mash if needed)
- Cottage cheese and soft cheese cubes
- Peeled potatoes (boiled, baked, mashed)
- Very small pieces of soft, well-cooked meats such as chicken

Finger Foods That Can Hurt Baby

These foods can cause your baby to choke:

- tortilla chips
- wieners, hot dogs
- olives
- bacon
- whole grapes or berries (OK if cut into small pieces)
- dried fruits, raisins
- hard candies
- peanut butter on a spoon
- popcorn
- nuts and seeds
- raw carrots

These foods can give your baby an upset tummy. They can cause gas, allergies and are hard to digest:

- corn
- leafy vegetables (lettuce, spinach, cabbage)
- cucumbers with seeds
- baked beans
- chocolate
- onions
- egg whites
- potato chips
- fish
- bacon

When Eating Habits Change

As your baby grows into a toddler, her eating habits and what she needs to eat will change. She will begin to feed herself, and may rebel against what you are serving. Toddlers often struggle with parents over food. All this is normal. Here are some common concerns about toddler eating habits.

The Concern	The "Why"
Toddler eats less; drinks less milk; refuses vegetables; seems to prefer cookies, bread, crackers.	Your child isn't growing nearly as fast in his second year. Expect a gain of only five or six pounds. Carbohydrates and sweets become more popular because toddlers like quick snacks which give quick energy. Try to avoid "empty" calorie foods and keep enough healthy foods available for meals and snacks.
Can't sit in a highchair for more than ten minutes.	A toddler's curiosity keeps her moving. Expect things and activities to be much more interesting than food. Toddlers are quick eaters, too; she can eat all the nutritious food she needs in ten minutes. Think ahead and offer her the most nutritious foods first!
Wants to decide for himself what, when and how he will eat.	The first steps toward independence are usually taken at mealtime. A toddler wants to make choices and decisions for himself. He shows this during mealtimes by refusing certain food, insisting that foods not touch or making other demands. Respect his need to make some decisions for himself.
Insists on eating only one food for every meal and snack.	Food fads are common as your toddler learns she has control over what she eats. She may stick with only one food for days and then switch to another. Be patient. This won't last and it won't hurt your child's health. Keep offering a variety of foods, but let her make the choice.
Mealtimes are messy.	Food is fun for experiments and toddlers like experiments. Food can be squashed, stacked, dropped, mixed. If this bothers you, make simple rules about playing with food. Pay attention and remove food when he is finished eating to prevent too much playing.
Evening meals are often a disaster.	Being tired, growing up and the changing sleep habits of a toddler can lead to a meltdown at dinner time. Try offering better breakfasts and lunches and plan nutritious early snacks if your child is too cranky to eat at the end of the day.

Avoiding Mealtime Madness

Avoiding struggles at mealtime isn't easy. It takes a lot of patience, but these are some of the first steps toward your child's independence. Babies and toddlers are busy learning and mealtime is a great time to experiment. They learn that food can be squashed, stacked, dropped and mixed! They learn about taste, texture and temperature. Take time to understand and plan ways to avoid some of the mealtime madness. Staying flexible and patient helps parents have fun with their baby during meals.

Kid Stuff

- No single food is absolutely necessary. There are always healthy substitutes to offer baby.
- Once your child is old enough, offer safe and nutritious foods he can eat using his spoon or his fingers.
- Serve small portions and let her ask for more, instead of insisting she eat all of a large portion.
- Respect your child's feeling of fullness—let him stop eating when he's ready.
- Offer choices of healthy foods at each meal, but don't insist that she eat everything offered.
- Serve your older baby some of what you eat, but you will need to adjust the salt, spices and seasonings.
- If your toddler prefers to quickly fill up on milk or juice and then turns down other foods, wait and bring out her drink midway through the meal.
- Don't use food as a reward or a bribe.
- Dessert should be considered part of the meal, not as a reward for eating the "good food." Serve healthy desserts like frozen yogurt or fruit.

Parent Stuff

- Be flexible in your expectations around food and babies. Toddlers especially want to decide for themselves what, when and how much and how often they eat.
- If you are worried about what your child is eating, keep track over a week or so of meals, not just one or two. Chances are things will even out over the course of time.
- Aim for mealtimes that are calm, upbeat family times. This can be a wonderful time to laugh and talk with your child. It's also a good time to listen to what baby has to say to you. (Try not to be rushed, turn off the TV, use kind words, etc.)
- Be a good role model for baby. Eat healthy foods and snacks.
- Don't get into food battles with your child. This helps you avoid power struggles now and possible eating problems later.

Hints for Peaceful Meals

- Drinking it is not the only way to get milk into a child's diet. Serve things that have milk as an ingredient— soups or macaroni and cheese, for example.
- Cereal for dinner and cheese cubes for breakfast are fine. Avoid the trap of specific foods only at specific meals.
- Fruits and vegetables have similar food value. Serve what your child will eat, but every once in awhile offer other options to try.

66

Chapter 5
Keeping Baby Well

Taking care of baby involves many things and one of them is keeping baby healthy. This section tells you what to expect at well-baby checkups, makes suggestions on ways to keep baby healthy, and gives information on treating minor illnesses at home.

Team Work: Baby's Doctor and You

New parents can rely on their health care clinic for a lot of support and information. It's important that you feel comfortable with the your baby's doctor and other clinic staff. When you're comfortable with the relationship, it's easier to ask questions, trust the answers and be a real team in keeping baby healthy. Here are some ways to build a good relationship.

Come to appointments with as much information as possible

Know your child's normal temperature, if and when any fever started, describe symptoms, general behavior and any changes you've noticed. All this helps the doctor understand your baby's health and give you the best information.

Write down any questions before the appointment

Jotting down questions means you won't forget them during the visit. This saves time for the doctor and it ensures that you get the information you need. Be prepared to make notes about the doctors answers and other information about baby's health.

Speak up

Be sure to ask any and all questions you have. Keep asking until you understand the answers.

Be willing to Try what the doctor says

Trust your doctor to give baby the best care she can. She has knowledge and experience in treating children. If she doesn't think medicine will help, listen to her. Or, if the doctor says to give baby medicine for a certain amount of time, follow his directions even if you think baby is better and doesn't need anymore medication. On the other hand, if the illness continues, or if you have any questions, be sure to call the doctor back.

If you can wait until office hours to call, do

Save after hours and night time calls for real emergencies. This can be hard for new parents. It often seems any change is worrisome and may be an emergency.

Know and follow the rules and polices of the clinic

This includes being on time, scheduling appointments, cancelling them if you can't make it and calling during office hours unless it's an emergency. The clinic staff will appreciate your cooperation and that helps you feel more comfortable. Everyone benefits—especially your baby.

Well-Baby Checkup: What To Expect

Babies need to have regular medical checkups. These checkups help you and baby's doctor know how baby is growing and changing. They also help discover any concerns about development. Well-baby checks are a good time for parents to ask questions about development and behavior, too. Always make a list of the questions or concerns you have so you can get them answered at the visit.

Each health care clinic will have a different routine for a well-baby checkup, but you can expect the following things to usually happen.

What About "Shots"?

Immunizations against childhood diseases such as polio, whooping cough, tetanus and others are part of a well-baby check. Recommendations for immunizations—both what types to get and when to get them—change as more research is done and new vaccines are developed. Your clinic will give you an up-to-date schedule for your baby. If you have any reservations or concerns about having your child immunized, discuss this with your doctor.

Doctor's questions
Your doctor will ask how well you, the baby and other family members are doing and ask questions about baby's sleeping, eating, and playing to get a picture of where baby is now.

Measuring and weighing
Baby will be weighed and her length and head circumference will be measured. The progress since birth will be recorded on her chart. Ask to be told this information so you can put it in your child's "baby book" or at-home medical file.

Vision and hearing checks
Simple tests for sight and hearing will be done to see if baby has normal sight and hearing.

Physical exam
The doctor or other health care professional will do a complete exam of baby. She will check heartbeat, pulse, stomach, hips, knees, feet, arms and hands for normal development, back and spine for any abnormalities, eyes, ears, nose, mouth and throat for anything unusual. She will check skin for rashes and bumps. She will feel underarms and abdomen or any swollen areas. She will check genitals, too. The doctor will look at overall movement and development. It may seem like a lot of poking and prodding—and baby may protest by crying—but a thorough exam at each visit can help prevent problems.

Remember to share medical and health information with baby's other parent and others who care for baby.

Information
The doctor or other staff will discuss baby's development now and what parents can expect in the next few weeks or months. They will tell you how to keep baby safe at this stage, too.

Your questions
Now is the time to ask and talk over all questions or concerns you may have about your baby's health and development.

Making Doctor's Visits Easier

Baby is right—being poked and prodded is no fun, but it is a necessary part of a well-baby check. Here are some ways to make the visit go more smoothly.

- Schedule visit for baby's best time of day, if possible. Avoid nap and feeding times, since a disruption of schedule can cause a fussy baby.
- Keep calm and upbeat, so your stress doesn't affect baby. Talk in a soothing, calm voice.
- Dress baby in easy-off clothes.
- Take baby's blanket to lay on table.
- A "lovey" or pacifier can comfort baby.
- Take a well-stocked diaper bag in case you have to wait.
- And don't worry if baby does cry. It's normal and the doctor and staff are used to babies' many moods.

Keeping Track of Baby's Health

Keep track of the information about your baby that you get at a well-baby checkup. This can help you see how your baby has grown and changed and can be a reference if you forget what you learned. Make copies of this form and fill it out at the doctor's office or when you get home. Keep this record in a safe place (your "baby book," a medical/health file, folder, etc.).

Date: _____

Baby's Name: _____ Age: _____

Weight: _____ Height: _____

Doctor/Clinic: _____

_____

Schedule next checkup for: _____

Is your baby at, below or above average in weight? In height?

_____

_____

What did the doctor notice about your baby's development?

_____

_____

_____

What did the doctor say about baby's diet?

_____

_____

Did baby get any immunizations? Which ones?

_____

_____

What reaction to the immunizations might be expected?

_____

_____

What did the doctor say about baby's development?

_____

_____

Did you learn more about keeping your baby safe?

_____

_____

Did you have any questions you forgot to ask?

_____

_____

70

Baby's Eyes and Ears

Your baby cannot tell you if she is having problems with hearing or vision. Parents can do some simple observations and activities to check baby's hearing and vision for any signs of a problem.

Hearing

If your baby notices noises and likes things that make noise, then your child can hear. But continue to check the child's hearing occasionally.

Watch your child closely

Does baby:

- turn toward a noise?
- change the look on her face when she hears a noise?
- stop what she is doing when she hears something?
- act surprised by a loud noise?
- wake up when there is a loud noise?
- seem afraid of some noises?

If you have any concerns about your child's sight or hearing, always tell baby's doctor or nurse. They will be able to test your baby's sight and hearing more completely.

Does baby like things that make noises?

Does your baby like to hear:

- your voice?
- her own voice? Does she babble or coo?
- toys that make music or noise?

Babies born with normal hearing can later have problems

Some things that can hurt baby's hearing are:

- ear infections
- being hit on the head
- falling on her head
- being near very loud noises

If one of these things happens to your baby, watch carefully for anything that indicates hearing problems.

Vision

If baby's eyes seem clear, with no sign of cloudiness, baby's eyes are probably fine. You can tell if she can see if she follows an object with her eyes.

Watch baby closely

These things may be a sign of a problem:

- Rubs eyes a lot.
- Eyes move too much.
- Doesn't seem to focus on things, even when they are up close.
- Squints frequently.
- Frowns a lot.
- One eye looks in toward nose.
- Has red or "watery" eyes
- Has sores on upper or lower eyelids (styes).
- Closes one eye a lot or puts a hand over one eye to see (usually an older child).

Babies that are born with normal eyesight can later have vision problems due to an illness or an accident. If your baby has a serious illness or an accident, watch for signs of a problem.

Baby Teeth

Baby teeth can appear as early as four months old or even earlier (some babies are born with teeth!). By age three, a child will have all of his baby teeth. Even though baby teeth aren't permanent, they must last a long time. Teeth are vulnerable to decay from their first appearance, so good tooth care is important from the very beginning.

Keeping Teeth Healthy

- A good diet helps prevent tooth decay. How long food stays on teeth is more significant than what and how much is eaten. That's why propping a bottle or letting a child have a bottle in bed are bad ideas. The liquid pools up in baby's mouth and stays against the teeth a long time. This causes tooth decay.

- Even before teeth appear, gently clean gums with a brush or wipe with your finger wrapped in a soft, clean cloth.

- Use a toothbrush designed for little children, with a small head and soft bristles. Replace every three months or when bristles looks worn. Every family member should have their own toothbrush.

- Skip toothpaste until your child can rinse and spit out leftover toothpaste. It's the "elbow grease"—the brushing—that actually cleans the teeth.

- Let your toddler brush her own teeth when she shows an interest, but you will need to finish the job until older.

Professional Care

- Recommendations vary as to when a child should first visit a dentist. When you decide to schedule the first visit depends on the condition of your toddler's teeth, doctor's advice, and your judgement.

- Any signs of abnormality—an open or un-aligned or "bad" bite, dark spots or uneven coloration on the teeth—require attention. Injury to mouth or teeth should be seen by dentist, too. Early attention to dental problems can prevent tooth decay and find any mouth irregularities that might interfere with speech development.

- Try a children's dentist. They have training in treating children, are familiar with their special needs, and are better prepared to handle the fears and short attention spans of little ones.

- Once teeth are in, a professional cleaning every six months will help prevent decay.

Hints

Some toddlers don't want any help when brushing teeth. Try these hints:

- Make it a game—"mistakenly" brush nose, ear, whatever.

- Take turns brushing. Let her brush your teeth with your own toothbrush. Then, you get to brush her's.

- Let him choose his own colorful toothbrushes and a toothpaste flavor he likes.

72

Yikes, Germs!

It's not possible to prevent all family illnesses. Everyone, including baby, is likely to get sick at one time or another. But there are certain things we can do that help prevent some illnesses.

There are many reasons we get sick, but germs are the main reason. Germs are everywhere, but are so tiny we can't see them without a microscope.

Germs are everywhere!

- In the air and on the ground
- Kitchens, bathrooms, bedrooms.
- Doctor's office, schools, child care centers, restaurants
- On towels, sponges, dish cloths
- Light switches, door knobs, stair railings, telephones
- On toys, dishes, furniture, clothes
- Around pets—fur, bowls, toys
- On other people (ourselves, too!)—Hands, mouths, hair.

Parents don't need to panic about germs and keep their families in sealed atmospheres because even with **all** the germs around, people aren't sick **all** the time. But, if we know how germs are spread, we can avoid those things that do make us ill.

How Germs Are Spread

- By coughing, sneezing
- Through touching, kissing, etc.
- Via shared things—telephones, cups, food, toothbrushes, etc.
- Putting things in mouth—hands, pencils, toys, etc.

Avoid Germs By:

- Avoid germs by washing hands often. (Also see page 74.)
- Covering mouth and nose when sneezing or coughing.
- Clean shared items regularly with bleach solution.
- Don't put things in mouth and keep children from putting things in theirs.
- Washing kitchen and bathroom counters, tubs, and sinks with bleach solution or antibacterial cleanser.

- If you have a dishwasher, it is good for sanitizing dishes, some small toys (watch out they don't melt!) and other small items.
- Change sponges and dish cloths regularly. Wash dirty ones in hot water and detergent. You can put sponges on the top rack of a dishwasher.
- Have a separate cup for each person in the bathroom or use disposable cups.
- Keep baby's play area, toys and other things clean.

Wash Those Hands

Handwashing is the single most important way you can prevent the spread of germs which cause common illnesses like colds. Knowing about and avoiding germs is one step that helps keep all of us healthy.

Steps to Help Stop the Spread of Germs

Washing hands

- Remove jewelry. Wet hands under warm running water.
- Rub hands together for at least 20 seconds using warm water and soap.
- Wash under fingernails, between fingers, back of hands and wrists. Use a brush for heavily soiled hands or before preparing food.
- Rinse hands well under running water.
- Dry thoroughly with a clean, dry towel (paper or cloth).
- Turn off water using the towel instead of bare hands.

When to wash your hands

- Before touching your baby.
- Before handling food or dishes.
- Before you eat or drink.
- After you use the bathroom.
- After you change a diaper.
- After you handle items soiled with body fluids or waste such as blood, drool, urine, stool or discharge from nose or eyes.
- After you clean up messes (blood, vomit, urine or stool).
- After you have touched a sick baby.
- After feeding or touching pets.
- And other times as needed.

When to wash your child's hands and face

- After he uses the bathroom.
- After she has touched someone who is sick.
- After he has played outside or in a public area.
- Before and after playing with moist items such as playdough.
- Before and after she eats.
- After he plays with pets.
- Whenever your instincts tell you to wash baby.

Items to Be Cleaned and Sanitized

Use a solution made by adding one tablespoon of bleach to one gallon of water. Put smaller items in this solution to clean and soak for a few minutes. Spray larger items with the solution (cribs, table tops, etc.). Do not rinse. Allow objects to air dry.

- Toys and equipment (for example: crib bars, walkers) — weekly or when soiled.
- Mouthed toys and objects — daily or when soiled.
- Highchair trays, table tops — before and after each use.
- Crib mattresses — weekly or when soiled.
- Kitchen and bathroom counters, tubs, sinks, toilets — when needed.
- Bathtub toys — weekly.

74

Is Baby Sick?

Since baby can't tell his parents when he is sick or how he feels, parents need to learn how to tell when baby is under the weather. Knowing the symptoms or signs of common childhood illness will help you know what to look for and know when or if it's time to call the doctor. If you do call, be prepared to describe what's going on with baby. Have the name and number of an open pharmacy so you can give them to the doctor if she needs to call in a prescription.

Parents' Intuition

You know your baby better than anyone else. If you think something "just isn't right" with baby, call the doctor. You may end up being reassured that everything is OK, but you may have found something that needs attention. Trust your feelings.

Think about baby's recent behavior and activities

- Is baby acting like he usually does or is something different? What is different about his behavior?
- Are there any symptoms of illness—fever, chills, fussing, pulling on ears…?
- When did the symptoms first appear?
- Did anything seem to trigger the symptoms?
- Does anything seem to make the symptoms better?
- What, if any, home remedies or over the counter medications have you tried? When? How did baby react?
- Has baby been exposed to anyone who is sick—someone with chicken pox or diarrhea, for example.
- Has baby been injured recently?

Each doctor's office or clinic will have guidelines about when to call. Check with your provider. Here are some general guidelines.

Call doctor immediately if baby:

- Has an axillary (underarm) temperature of 101° F for more than 12 to 24 hours. (See page 78.)
- Has diarrhea and/or has vomited more than once.
- Is in obvious pain.
- Cannot be comforted.

Wait until doctor's office is open to call if baby:

- Has a temperature which is rising, **but** is brought down to 101° F by non-aspirin pain/fever medication.
- Has a cough.
- Has symptoms that have continued for several days.

Other things to check

- **Temperature** — Take baby's axillary temperature if she feels warm to touch. (See page 78.)
- **Breathing** — Is he having difficulty breathing? Is he coughing, or breathing rapidly?
- **Nose** — Is it runny or stuffy? Is there a discharge? What color is the discharge? Does stuffy nose prevent baby from breastfeeding or drinking from a bottle?
- **Coughing** — Any mucus or dry, hacking cough? Does it keep baby from sleeping or eating?
- **Behavior** — Any changes in normal behavior? Sleeping more or less than usual? Activity level the same, more or less? Crying more than usual? Does cry sound different? Appetite the same or eating less? Is baby drinking well?
- **Skin** — Any changes in color? Is it warm and moist or cool and clammy? Spots or rashes?
- **Eyes** — Do eyes look different than usual? Any discharge?
- **Ears** — Is she poking or pulling at her ears? Any discharge?
- **Vomiting/diarrhea** — How often and what does it look like? Any changes in bowel movements, urination normal?
- **Movement** — Can baby move normally? Any trembling, chills, difficulty moving or stiffness?

Sick Baby: Information for the Doctor

This form can help you gather the information the doctor or clinic may ask when you call for an appointment or advice about a sick baby.

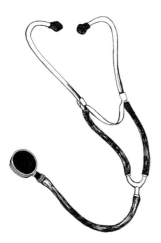

Baby's name: _____   Birth date: _____

Weight: _____   Height: _____

Baby's medical record number: _____

Doctor/clinic: _____   Phone: _____

Pharmacy: _____   Phone: _____

When did baby begin to get sick? _____

Axillary (underarm) temperature? (Take before giving medicine.) _____

Appetite? _____

Vomiting? How often? _____

Diarrhea? How often? _____

Urinating normally? _____

Coughing? When, how much? _____

Runny nose? Color, amount? _____

Skin problems? (rash, etc.) _____

Pain? Where, how much? _____

Is each symptom getting better or worse? _____

_____

What have you already done for baby? _____

_____

Is baby taking any medicine now? _____

Does baby have any health problems? (allergies, asthma)? _____

_____

Additional questions:

Is anyone else in the family sick? _____

_____

Do you want to see a doctor or are you calling for advice? _____

Other notes:

_____

_____

_____

_____

Baby's Medicine Cabinet

Baby can get sick with little warning. It can happen any time of day or night. With some simple supplies on hand, you can respond to baby's illness and make him feel better.

Items to Have On Hand

Item	Information
❑ Non-aspirin pain/ fever medication*	_____
❑ Cough medicine for infants*	_____
❑ Nasal decongestant	_____
❑ Diaper rash ointment*	_____
❑ Syrup of Ipecac* (to start vomiting in case of poisoning)	_____
❑ Other: _____	
	_____
	_____

*Talk to your doctor before giving these medications to baby (what brand, how much, how often and more).

❑ Thermometer	_____
❑ Vaporizer (cold air)	_____
❑ Bulb syringe	_____
❑ Rubbing alcohol	_____
❑ Petroleum jelly	_____
❑ Bandages, gauze pads and tape	_____
❑ Cottonballs	_____
❑ Other: _____	
	_____
	_____

Think Safety
Always keep medicines out of baby's reach.

Tips for Giving Medicine

- Before baby gets sick, ask your doctor about over-the-counter medicines he recommends.

- Follow all directions carefully—when, how much, whether to give before or after eating.

- Always put the cover back on the bottle and store as directed—in refrigerator or cabinet. Otherwise it could spill, spoil, or evaporate.

- If medicine comes with a measuring spoon or dropper, use it to measure the amount you are giving baby.

- Put medicine directly into baby's mouth, rather than mixing it in a bottle or cup of milk or juice. Baby may not drink it all and won't get a full dose of medicine.

- **Never** give your baby anyone else's medicine, even if it worked for the other person.

- **Complete all medicine prescribed.** Do not change dosage or stop without talking to baby's doctor.

- When you give baby medicine, say some encouraging words. Expect baby to take medicine well. If you get tense or make a face, it's likely your baby will, too.

Baby's Got a Fever: Axillary Temperature

There will come the day when you will need to take baby's temperature. It's best and safest for parents to take the axillary, or underarm temperature, instead of taking it rectally or orally. A child needs to be four or five years old to have temperature taken orally. Rectal temperature taking requires practice, and few babies want to go along with that! The axillary temperature is slightly less accurate than either oral or rectal, but it's good enough to determine whether or not baby has a fever. Be sure to tell your doctor that you're reporting the axillary temperature.

Keep baby calm for half an hour before taking temperature. Crying or screaming could make a slight fever higher.

Shake thermometer (if using a mercury type) until it reads 96° F or less. Turn on a digital thermometer, if using that type.

Remove baby's shirt so no clothing is between skin and thermometer. Be sure armpit is dry.

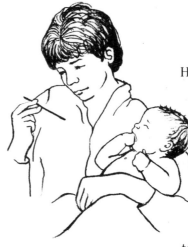

Place bulb end of thermometer well up into the armpit. Hold the arm snugly down over it and press baby's arm against his side.

Hold this position for at least four or five minutes, if possible. Entertain baby while you wait— sing songs, read a story.

Read the thermometer— 98.6° F is a normal temperature for an axillary reading.

When you report the temperature to the doctor's office, be sure to tell them it's axillary.

When to Call Your Doctor

Parents are often very concerned when baby has a fever. Talk to your doctor about when to call about baby's fever, but here are **some general guidelines.**

Call immediately if:
- Fever is over 101° F axillary.
- Baby has a convulsion or seizure.
- Baby is crying inconsolably and it's not colic. Cries as if in pain.
- Baby is whimpering, nonresponsive or limp.
- Baby has purple spots anywhere on skin.
- Baby is having difficulty breathing.

Call as soon as practical if:
- Baby seems dehydrated.
- Baby's behavior is uncharacteristic.
- A low fever suddenly spikes up.
- Fever isn't brought down by non-aspirin pain/fever medication.
- Fever lasts more than three days.

Treating Minor Illnesses

Parents can help baby feel better as he gets over a minor illness by doing some of these things. Be sure to talk to your doctor before giving medicine.

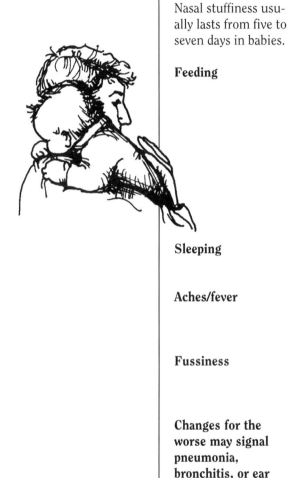

The Problem	Ways to Help Baby Feel Better
Common cold Nasal stuffiness usually lasts from five to seven days in babies.	
Feeding	Give a lot of liquids; don't worry about whether baby eats solid food. Let baby decide how hungry she is.
	If stuffiness prevents nursing, remove congestion from nose with a bulb syringe. Wrap baby tightly (arms included) in a blanket. Place baby's feet on your lap, head between your legs, baby's feet towards your waist. Hold baby with one hand. Use bulb syringe to gently draw out matter with bulb in other hand.
Sleeping	Raise head of mattress slightly by putting a blanket under mattress. A cold air vaporizer can help.
Aches/fever	Check with your doctor about if, when and how to use non-aspirin medication. A decongestant may be prescribed when the baby is six months old.
Fussiness	Baby may need a simpler routine and more sleep. Taking baby outside is OK, but may not be enjoyable for either you or baby.
Changes for the worse may signal pneumonia, bronchitis, or ear infection	**Call your doctor. Baby must be seen by doctor because an antibiotic is used to fight infection.**

(continued)

The Problem	Ways to Help Baby Feel Better

Ear infections

Sometimes accompany a cold, but not always. Pain may not seem to be inside the ear.

Marked by:
- crying
- ear rubbing
- fever
- irritability, difficult behavior
- hearing loss caused by fluids behind the eardrum

If baby wakes in the middle of the night with ear pain, treat with non-aspirin pain reliever until morning, then call the doctor. If baby has an infection, she will need antibiotics that only a doctor can prescribe. Be sure to give all of the medicine that the doctor prescribes, even if it seems baby is better.

Ear infections often come back, even after taking all the medicine. Watch for symptoms. Go back to the doctor for a recheck after antibiotics are done. Watch for any signs of hearing loss.

Diarrhea

Forceful elimination of **four or more** loose, watery stools a day. (This is different for breastfed babies who may have five to eight watery, curdy stools.) Causes are same as for vomiting.

General rule is to let tummy and intestines rest so they can heal.

If your doctor doesn't give you a schedule, here is one:

- Fluids (as recommended for vomiting) for the first 24 hours.

- If stools decrease in number and increase in consistency, reintroduce solids; rice cereal, bananas, applesauce, crackers. Do not give dairy products or citrus fruits.

- Begin regular diet.
  Reintroduce dairy products last. If baby slips back into diarrhea, call your doctor.

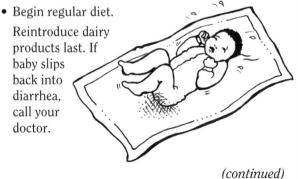

(continued)

The Problem	Ways to Help Baby Feel Better
Vomiting May be a reaction to new food or intolerance of new food. Or may be caused by a virus, other infection or by more serious problems.	Baby should continue taking liquids but wait until vomiting stops to feed baby solid foods. Wait two hours after vomiting, then give room temperature, clear liquids by teaspoonfuls. Liquids may be water, de-fizzed 7-Up®, Jello® with twice as much water as usual, weak tea, half apple juice/half water. Use rehydration fluids like Pedialyte® or Infalyte® if recommended by baby's doctor. If breastfeeding, continue to give baby breast milk because it is gentle on baby's tummy and is easy to digest.
Diarrhea may follow if caused by a virus.	See suggestions for treating diarrhea.
If vomiting lasts more than six to eight hours.	Call your doctor.
If vomiting is projectile:	Call your doctor.

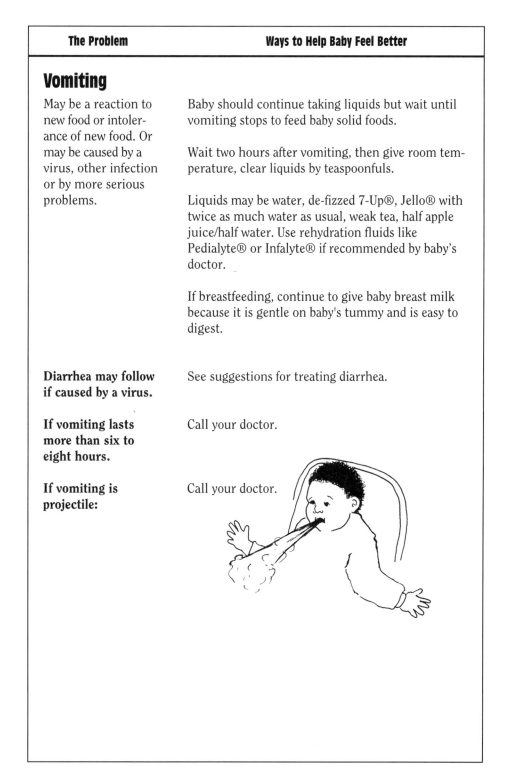

Your Notes

You can use this page to make notes about things you've learned, questions you have, milestones reached, and more. It can be a record of some of the events in your life as a new parent—your dreams, memories, concerns, hopes, and plans. Or perhaps this is a place to write down and celebrate baby's changes, growth and development —that first tooth, first word, first step...

Chapter 6
Keeping Baby Safe

Keeping children safe from accidents is one of the responsibilities of parenthood. Children need your help to avoid accidents and stay safe. This chapter helps parents with childproofing the home for their growing child, talks about accident prevention, and gives some simple first aid techniques to handle minor bumps and scrapes.

Twenty-Five Ways to Keep Baby Safe

Whenever you're looking at ways to childproof or keep baby safe, always think about your environment, what your baby is doing now and what baby might do next. Look over these simple suggestions, do a check of your home take other safety steps as you see the need.

Always stay with baby

Don't leave baby alone—in a car, at home, near water and more. For example, if the phone rings, let it go, or take baby with you to answer.

Don't shake baby or play rough

It's easy to hurt a baby accidentally. Shaking a baby can cause dangerous head and neck injuries or even kill baby.

Always hold baby during feedings.

Baby needs your touch and propping bottles can cause ear infections and tooth decay.

Keep small objects out of reach

Check baby's area for things like string, balloons, rubber bands, coins, pills, pebbles or similar things baby could put in his mouth.

Keep all cords away from baby

Curtain, phone, hair dryer cords, and other dangling cords are dangerous. Do not tie baby's pacifier to a cord around his neck or near him. It could strangle him.

Keep sharp objects away from baby

Scissors, razors, pencils, clothes hangers, knives and more.

Put away or throw away all plastic bags

Plastic bags can cause suffocation if baby swallows pieces or they cover his nose or mouth. Keep these out of babies reach. Before throwing plastic bags, tie them in several knots.

Do not hold baby while eating or drinking hot food or smoking cigarettes

A spill or dropped ash could burn your baby.

Be careful while cooking

Don't allow your baby to roam the kitchen while you're cooking. Keep baby in a secure place where you can see and hear each other. Turn pan handles to the middle of the stove.

Block all stairways at the top and bottom

Use securely attached gates so baby cannot move them.

Avoid space heaters

Space heaters burn little fingers and can cause a fire. Keep baby away with a gate or barrier. Don't let cloth, paper or other flammable items get near the heater.

Be careful when using electric fans

Little fingers can fit through the covers. Baby may poke a pencil or other object in fan.

Check things that touch baby's skin

Check the temperature of bath water, baby's food and more. These things can burn baby's.

Never let baby suck or eat any part of a plant.

Many common indoor and outdoor plants are poisonous. And even if they are not poisonous, they can cause upset tummies.

Check toys for safety

Toys should not have small parts, sharp edges or broken pieces. Check page 90 for more on toy safety.

(continued)

84

Twenty-Five Ways to Keep Baby Safe *(continued)*

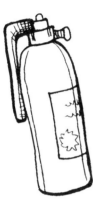

Be careful of fire

Keep all matches, lighters, lit cigarettes, candles, incense and other fire hazards out of baby's reach. Have working smoke detectors and a fire extinguisher in your home. Make a fire safety plan for your family and home. If you would like suggestions about fire safety plans for families, call your neighborhood fire station for information.

Keep poisons away from baby

Medicines, cleaning items, rodent poisons, insect repellents, paints, vitamins, gasoline, cigarettes, pet supplies, cosmetics and more should be kept out of reach or locked up so baby cannot get into them. Keep all drugs and alcohol away from baby.

Tips about safe baby equipment are on pages 26-28.

Never leave baby near water of any kind

Don't leave baby alone in the bathtub. Drain water from tub as soon as bath is finished. Look for other water sources, too, like open toilet seats, cleaning buckets and wading pools. Babies can drown in as little as 1" of water.

Make transportation safe by always using a car seat

Don't let baby be near things that contain lead

Lead is harmful to babies and adults. The most common source of household lead comes from things that were painted before the 1970s—toys, baby equipment, furniture, woodwork, walls and more. If your home is possibly painted with lead-based paint, keep baby from chewing on window sills, cribs and other similar surfaces. Tiny bits of lead-based paint may also be found in household dust that can be breathed into our bodies. Vacuum, sweep, dust and mop your home often if this is a concern for you. For information call 1-800-LEAD-FYI.

Keep baby's sleeping area safe

Crib bars should be no more than three fingers apart. Mattress should fit tightly with no gaps between the mattress and walls of crib.

Babies can get hurt by rolling of adult size beds. Don't leave baby alone on a bed.

Use a mattress on the floor, place a drawer from a dresser on the floor, or use a strong box if a crib is not available.

Keep all electrical appliances away from water

Don't leave hair dryers, radios or other things plugged in or use them near water. Baby could pull the item into the water, which could electrocute her.

Use safe baby equipment

Make sure high chairs and infant seats have safety straps.

If your playpen has fabric mesh, don't use it if the mesh tears easily. If the playpen has wood slats, make sure they are no more than three fingers apart.

Cover all electrical outlets

Use heavy tape or commercial outlet covers to keep baby from poking his fingers or objects in the outlets.

Keep cabinets latched.

Kitchen and bathroom cupboards or cabinets should be latched with childproof latches to keep baby from getting at the dangers inside.

Keeping Up With Baby

As baby grows and develops, his new mobility and other skills can increase the chance of an accident. By understanding how baby grows and changes and at what ages he is likely to do certain things, you can childproof and plan ahead for ways to keep baby safe. Keep in mind that babies at this age really need someone with them who is watching out for their safety at all times.

What Baby Has Learned	Possible Accidents	Safety Steps to Take
Moves around in crib by rolling, wiggling or pushing with legs	Could get stuck between mattress and side of crib	Make sure mattress fits snugly and bars are less than 2-3/8 inches apart.
Grabs or bats at things	Could pull something down on himself	Keep all objects that could hurt baby out of reach. Stop using tablecloths and placemats.
Wants to put everything in her mouth	Could choke	Keep all small objects out of reach. Check baby's area often and carefully. (Anything that can fit in a toilet paper tube is too small to have around baby.)
Rolls over	Could roll off couch, bed, changing table, down stairs	Don't leave baby alone. Use safety belts and child safety gates when necessary.
Sits alone for one minute	Could fall over	Don't leave child sitting alone.
Feeds self	Could choke if too much or unsafe food is put in mouth	Give baby small pieces of safe foods. Always stay with baby at mealtimes.
Bangs objects together	Could smash fingers or cause something dangerous to break	Give baby lightweight, flexible, soft playthings. Make sure she can't reach things made of glass or hard, brittle plastic.

(continued)

Keeping Up With Baby *(continued)*

What Baby Has Learned	Possible Accidents	Safety Steps to Take
Climbs	Could fall from a high place	Keep any climbing helpers—chairs, etc.—away from windows, tables, counters or other unsafe places for baby to climb.
Stands by pulling and holding onto furniture	Could fall or pull furniture over on self	Remove tablecloths, lamps and other things that could be pulled and fall on baby. Make sure furniture is sturdy and stable. Clear floor area of toys, rugs, newspapers, shoes and other things that could trip baby. Stay with baby.
Crawls and walks holding furniture	Could fall or get stuck in tight spots Baby can get around better and this increases chances to find additional things that are dangerous	Never leave baby alone. Childproof with safety gates, outlet covers and more. Get down to baby's eye level and check for dangers. Clear floor of things that could cause falls. (Toys, rugs, newspapers, shoes and other things that could trip baby.)

Foods with hard sticks in them, such as lollipops and frozen treats, are not safe for small children. Baby could fall and the stick could hurt her mouth or choke her.

Childproofing For Baby

Even the smallest baby needs his parents help to keep him safe from harm. Look around for hazards and remove them so baby can't get hurt. Go room by room with this list and make changes to keep baby safe.

Child safety means being alert. Babies develop very quickly and are soon able to do things that we may not expect. Never leave baby alone on a couch, changing table or near water of any kind.

Bedrooms and changing area

- If using a changing table, always fasten safety straps to keep baby from rolling off.
- Check for items baby can pull on herself from nearby shelves.
- Outlets covered.
- Childproof latches on drawers.
- Be sure all hanging pictures and any objects on dressers or bookshelves near crib are out of baby's reach.
- Keep furniture baby could climb on—chairs, tables, diaper pails, toys—away from windows.
- Securely close diaper pail every time.
- Don't empty pockets of coins, paper clips, pens where baby can reach. Keep closet doors and drawers shut.

Crib safety

- No missing hardware, rough edges, etc.
- Mattress fits snugly.
- Corner posts/slats meet standards.
- No soft bedding (pillow, fluffy quilts).

Living room

- Outlets covered.
- No curtain or lamp cords within reach.
- Check for choking hazards— small things, plastics, foam rubber, etc.
- Sharp table edges are cushioned or are moved.
- Put knickknacks and breakables out of reach.
- Keep TV, VCR and stereo equipment out of reach.
- Don't use glass-topped tables.
- Look for loose nails, staples or tacks on all upholstered furniture.
- Never leave lamp light bulb sockets empty. Screw all bulbs in tightly.
- Remove or secure bookshelves that may topple over on baby.
- Keep furniture baby could climb on—chairs, tables, diaper pails, toys—away from windows.

Kitchen

- Garbage in covered container.
- No plastic bags or wrap where baby can find. Tie into knots before throwing away.
- Use a sturdy highchair that has safety belts or straps.
- Cook on back burners. Turn pot handles out of baby's reach. Stove knobs covered or removed.
- Keep a fire extinguisher handy and know how to use it.
- Childproof latches on all cupboards and drawers.
- Dishwasher door kept latched.
- Phone cords out of reach.

(continued)

Childproofing For Baby *(continued)*

Bathroom

- Baby never left alone near water.
- Cover toilet seat, drain bathtub after use.
- Childproof latches on all cupboards and drawers.
- Water heater set no higher than 120° F.
- Nonskid mats in tub, shower and on floor.
- Plastic bottles and cups—not glass.
- Razors, medicines, cosmetics, vitamins, aftershave/perfume, shampoo, cleaners and mouthwash are locked up or stored out of baby's reach.
- Electric appliances (hair dryers, etc.) unplugged and put away out of reach.
- Never use electric appliances around water.
- Keep door closed when not in use.

Other

- All household chemicals, cleaners, paints, pesticides and more locked up.
- Tools, hardware, rakes, etc. out of reach. Store power tools unplugged.
- Iron and ironing boards put away after use.
- Washer and dryer doors kept closed.
- No buckets of water, open toilet seats, wading pools, etc. around for baby to get into.
- Litter box and pet food out of reach.

- Smoke detectors and carbon monoxide detectors installed and checked as recommended.
- Safety gates where needed.
- Install window guards or locks that let windows open only a few inches.
- If you believe your child will be near an electrically opening garage door, be sure to check it for safety. Could it close and crush baby or does the door go back up if an abject the size of baby is in it's path? Be sure automatic garage door meets current safety standards. Make sure garage door opener's remote controller is out of your child's reach.

There may be different hazards in your home. Take a good look from baby's eye level. Keep in mind that as a baby grows, childproofing must change to meet her new abilities.

© Meld 1999 • 612-332-7563

Toy Safety for Little Ones

Toys are a big part of every child's life. Buy only toys which meet these guidelines and check gift toys for safety, too. Keep in mind that cheap toys are no bargain. They break easily, which disappoints child and can be dangerous.

Babies put everything in their mouths. They don't know or remember what is unsafe. Be sure toys have no small parts that can come off and be swallowed.

For Infants and Toddlers

Dolls and stuffed animals

Remove all bows and bells that can be swallowed. Choose dolls with stitched-on features rather than buttons and plastic parts that may be bitten or pulled off.

Crib toys

Never attach toys to an infant's crib with any kind of ribbon, string or elastic. Babies could be strangled.

Soft but safe

Soft toys such as rattles, squeakers and small dolls should not be small enough to be squished and jammed into a baby's mouth.

Old toys

Older toys may not meet today's safety standards.

Wall hangings and mobiles

Remove mobiles and any other hanging objects when an infant is able to touch them. Decorative hangings near or on the crib are interesting for newborns to look at, but they are a safety hazard once a child can reach out and touch them.

Foam toys

Avoid foam toys. Pieces bitten off can be swallowed. These can be a choking hazard.

Push-and-straddle toys

Make sure older baby can touch the ground when sitting on a riding toy. Toy should be not be easy to tip over.

Toy storage

Use toy chests that have removable lids. Open shelves and containers are safer for babies and offer easier access instead of the jumble of a deep toy chest. Check to make sure shelves can't be toppled over onto baby.

Balloons and Plastics

Never let baby play near or with balloons and plastic wrappings. Balloons are the leading cause of death by suffocation for children. Children can choke on and be suffocated by an uninflated balloon, a piece of a broken balloon or by plastic package wrapping.

(continued)

Toy Safety for Little Ones *(continued)*

Age labels and small parts

Pay attention to age recommendations on toys. "Not for children under age three" usually means there are small parts. These toys are unsafe for little ones—no matter how smart they may be! They are unsafe for some three and four-year-olds who put things in their mouth, too.

Batteries

Most infant and toddler toys don't need batteries. But if they are needed, batteries should be inaccessible to child. This may mean it's difficult for parents to change the batteries, but that's OK.

Quality control

Run your fingers around edges of toys to be sure there are no rough, sharp or splintery, hidden edges. Check for parts that can catch or pinch little fingers.

For Mixed Ages

When children of different ages play together, set up some safety rules about toys with small parts. Older children's toys often have small parts that younger babies might choke on. Keep these toys out of baby's reach.

Older children need to have a place where they can play and work on activities so younger children and babies can't get at the pieces and be hurt by or destroy the project or play activity.

Always supervise playtime when young children and babies play near each other. Accidents can happen very quickly.

All toys should be checked from time to time for broken parts, sharp edges or open seams. Occasionally clearing out the clutter of too many playthings can bring to the surface old toys that may have been forgotten.

Let's Play Outside: Safety Tips

Keeping children safe —
both at home and while
you're out and about—is
an important responsibil-
ity of parenthood. Much
of the information on
childproofing, first aid
and other safety issues
found on previous pages
also work when you and
baby are outside your
home. Here are a few
things to think about for
ways to keep baby safe
when you go out to play.

**One on the
best ways to keep
baby safe is to live
safely yourself.**

Here are some ideas:

- Avoid dangerous situa-
  tions, places and people
  whenever possible.

- Keep doors locked when
  at home.

- Follow traffic rules
  yourself.

- Use helmets, seat belts,
  and other safety devices.

- Keep guns under lock
  and key.

Water Safety

- Don't leave your little
  one unsupervised or
  out of sight near any
  water—wading pool,
  bathtub, swimming
  pool, beach, bucket
  of water. A child can
  drown in as little as
  one inch of water.

- Drain water from
  wading pools and turn
  upside down when not
  in use.

- Remove all toys from
  swimming pool when
  not in use. An unsuper-
  vised child may try to
  get them and drown.

- Don't consider child
  "drown-proof" because
  he is wearing a flota-
  tion device (life jacket).

Playground Safety

- Never leave your toddler
  alone on playground
  toys. Always stay next
  to her to help guide
  and keep her safe.

- Be sure play area and
  equipment is appropri-
  ate for the age of your
  baby or toddler.

- Be sure everything
  is safe:

  – No sharp edges,
    corners or exposed
    moving parts (swing
    chains are covered,
    for example). No
    rust or corrosion
    on metal parts.

  – Swings and slides
    are firmly anchored
    and sized for very
    small children.

  – Swings are made of
    canvas, rubber or
    light plastic, not
    wood or metal.

  – Surface under the
    equipment is cush-
    ioned—rubber mat-
    ting, sand or wood
    chips—not asphalt
    or concrete.

Burns and
Bug Bites

- Sunburn can be dan-
  gerous. Infants and
  toddlers should always
  wear a hat in the sun.
  Use sunblock on babies
  over six months old.
  Ask your doctor to
  recommend a brand.

- Always check for hot
  surfaces on playground
  equipment, outdoor
  toys, car seats and
  more.

- "Bug spray" to keep
  biting insects away is
  important in some
  areas. Ask your doctor
  to recommend a brand
  that is safe for children.
  Follow the directions
  on the package on how
  to apply.

Accidents and Stress

Childproofing and being alert to where baby is and what she is doing go a long way to prevent accidents. However, there are times when parents can't be alert. When you are tired, stressed, or distracted, the chances of an accident are higher. There are other times when accidents are more likely, too.

Knowing about stress areas helps you to be aware of possible dangerous times and to take steps to make baby's world safe.

Each person has a different reaction to stress. Some people have headaches, some get an upset stomach. Still others "take it out" on those around them, including children. Parents who find positive ways to handle stress can help families cope with difficult situations and with everyday life. Here are a few ideas that some parents have used to relieve stress.

Accidents Happen More Often When:

- You and/or your child is hungry, tired or not feeling well.

- There isn't a child-proofed place for baby to play and explore.

- The relationship between the adults in the home is tense and unhappy.

- When a your baby is in a new place—for instance, visiting friends, at a new babysitter's, after moving to a new home.

- Other family members are ill or at the center of parent's attention.

- Your family is rushed.

- You overestimate the ability of your child to protect herself.

- Baby is in the care of an unfamiliar person or of a brother or sister too young to be responsible.

- You're always very worried about your young child's safety and make the child feel inadequate.

- Someone in the home is using alcohol or drugs.

Five Minutes Peace: Stress Relievers

Escape for awhile
Give yourself a "time out." Find someone you trust to babysit. Then take a walk, listen to music, call a friend, whatever works for you.

Take action
Relieve some stress by talking, exercising, singing, trying a relaxation technique, asking for help or something else that works for you.

Be realistic
Stop for a minute, take a deep breath and look at the situation again. How bad is it, really? Is this the very worst that can happen? Will you even remember this in a year?

Humor
Laughter is a great stress reliever. Promise yourself that every day you will find something to laugh out loud about.

Make a change
Even small changes can relieve stress and help us see things from a new angle. Turn off radio or TV, for example. The quiet may be just what you need.

Avoid chemicals/alcohol
It may seem that these substances can make you more calm or relaxed, but in the long run, they will cause even greater stress.

Ease up
Go easy with criticism of yourself and others. Let go of the idea that things need to be perfect or to go exactly as you planned.

Keep it simple
Take one thing at a time. Break big problems or chores down to smaller steps. Do you really need to do it all, on time and in a certain way?

Play
You're never too old! It's good for your body, your brain and your attitude. Play with your friends, play on your own and **especially, take time to play with your child!**

Being Prepared for Emergencies

No one wants to be faced with an emergency involving a child, but an accident or illness can happen. You can react more calmly in any emergency if you rehearse what you would do, including who and when to call, how you would go to the emergency room or doctor's office, neighbors or relatives who might be able to help, and ways to help you keep yourself calm. Talk it all over so you are prepared to act quickly if you have to.

Ideas to Think About

- Talk to baby's doctor about when it's best to call the clinic or go to the emergency room or call 911. Recommendations may vary depending on time of day, day of week and nature of injury or illness.

- Keep first aid supplies handy, along with other supplies you might need (see the list on page 93).

- Post emergency numbers near each phone in the house. Include doctors' numbers, pharmacy, emergency numbers (e.g., 911 and Poison Control), taxi numbers, and numbers of family or friends you can call in an emergency. Keep a similar list in baby's diaper bag. (See page 100.)

- Know the quickest way to the emergency room, doctor's office, pharmacy and other emergency help.

- Keep some cash in a safe place so you have cab fare in case of an emergency.

- Learn infant CPR and rescue breathing and keep your skills up-to-date. The Red Cross can tell you where to get the training.

- Learn to handle emergencies calmly. You can best help your child by calling for help quickly, knowing basic first aid procedures and by staying calm and using a soothing voice.

- Your love and kisses can go a long way in comforting baby when he's upset by a minor injury.

Baby's First Aid Kit

Most baby and toddler injuries are minor—small cuts, bumped heads. Parents can usually take care of these "boo-boos" with first aid supplies, basic information, sympathy, and lots of kisses.

A well-stocked, child-proofed first aid kit is a handy thing to have at home. Keep items together in a box or other container stored safely away from little children. Make a smaller, child-safe travel kit to go with you on outings, too.

Hint:
A frozen sponge or a plastic bag of frozen peas works great as a cold pack.

Supplies to Have On Hand

Item	Information
❑ Non-aspirin pain/fever medication*	_____
❑ Syrup of Ipecac*	_____
❑ Antibacterial hand wipes*	_____
❑ Antiseptic ointment*	_____
❑ Hot/cold packs	_____
❑ Rubbing alcohol	_____
❑ Bandages in assorted sizes*	_____
❑ Gauze pads and tape*	_____
❑ Triangular bandage or bandana*	_____
❑ Thermometer	_____
❑ Small scissors*	_____
❑ Tweezers*	_____
❑ Sewing needles*	_____
❑ Matches to sterilize needle* (put in waterproof container such as a film canister)	_____
❑ Nasal bulb syringe	_____
❑ Tissues*	_____
❑ Medicine doser (syringe, dropper, spoon)	_____
❑ Emergency information and money for phone calls*	_____
❑ Small flashlight/extra batteries	_____
❑ Other: _____	_____
_____	_____

*Include in child-safe travel kit.

First Aid Basics

Parents can take care of many simple problems at home. Help yourself to be ready to help baby by asking your doctor for information, taking a first aid class and/or getting a good, basic, illustrated health care and first aid book for you to have at home.

The following are some very simple suggestions for ways to take care of baby when accidents happen. Talk to your doctor to get more background information.

Keep in mind that your hugs, kisses and calm, sympathetic voice goes a long way in helping your baby when he is hurt and scared. Be generous with this good medicine.

Cuts and Scrapes	• Gently sponge off scraped area with a clean cloth or gauze pad and soap. Apply pressure to stop bleeding. Cover with bandage or gauze pad and adhesive tape. • Treat small cuts as you do scrapes. Put bandage on cut so it holds edges of cut together. Larger cuts should be seen by a doctor to see if stitches are needed. Cuts on face should be seen by doctor.
Minor burns	• Immediately run cool water on the area for ten minutes. Check to see if the burn is still painful. If it is, keep the burn covered with cool water for more time. • Any burn on a child less than one year old should be seen by a doctor.
Bumped head	• Apply cold compress or ice pack to area. • Watch for signs of severe head injury: convulsions, vomiting, loss of consciousness, dizziness, indentation in skull, unequal pupil size, sleepiness. Call doctor immediately if any of these signs appear.
Splinters	• Wash area with soap and water. Numb with ice pack. If sliver is completely embedded, try to work it loose with sewing needle sterilized with alcohol or flame of a match. If end is visible, try to pull it out with a sterilized tweezers. • Can't get the sliver out? Leave it be for a few days. Eventually baby's body will work the splinter out on it's own. Keep checking though for possible infection. • When sliver is out, thoroughly wash area again.
Insect bites	• Wash site of minor stings and bites with soap and water. Apply ice pack or cold compress. Apply calamine or other anti-itch medicine to itchy bites. • Watch for signs of a serious reaction: severe pain or swelling, difficulty breathing. Call doctor immediately signs occur.

(continued)

First Aid Basics *(continued)*

Bites *(human and animal)*	• Wash area with soap and warm water for 15 minutes. Try not to move affected part. Control bleeding with pressure. Cover with sterile gauze and antiseptic ointment. • All bites that break the skin should be seen by a doctor.
Bruises	• Apply cold pack for up to half an hour. • If skin is broken, treat as a cut or scrape.
Puncture wounds	• Soak injury in hot, soapy water for 15 minutes. Cover wound with antiseptic ointment and bandage or gauze and adhesive tape. If needed, apply a hot or cold pack (whichever gives the most comfort). • Don't remove any object that is sticking out of the wound (stick or nail, for example). Your doctor needs to do this. • Check with doctor to see if tetanus booster is up to date and for other information.
Mouth injuries	• Apply cold pack to the injury. • If cut gapes open or won't stop bleeding after 15 minutes, call doctor. • If bleeding doesn't stop, squeeze sides of cut together with gauze or clean cloth. • Punctures from a sharp object (pencil or stick, for example) or injuries to the soft palate should be seen by doctor.
Something in eye	• If you can see the object, use a moistened cottonball to remove object. Or, rinse eye with clean, running of water. • Call your doctor if you can't get the object out or if baby is still uncomfortable.

Foods with hard sticks in them, such as lollipops and frozen treats, can be dangerous for small children. Baby could fall and the stick could hurt her mouth or choke her.

Calling for Help

Talk to your doctor about when to call the clinic, when to go to the emergency room or when to call for emergency help. Become familiar with life-threatening situations which demand immediate help.

Call 911 when your child...

You do not need coins to dial 911 from a pay phone.

- is having a problem breathing, is turning blue or choking.
- is bleeding and it can't be stopped.
- is unconscious or unresponsive.

These are life-threatening problems and your doctor's office may not be able to help.

Call a doctor immediately (day or night) when your child...

- has been burned and skin is off.
- has swallowed a poison. (Call Poison Control if your area has that service.)
- has a broken bone.
- is knocked unconscious.
- is having a seizure.
- has a temperature over 103° F which can't be brought down.
- is unresponsive and is not eating.

These problems are urgent and will not get better without medical attention.

98

Emergency: First Steps

If your baby has had a serious injury or accident, here are some things to do right away. Remember to try to stay calm, communicate clearly with those you call for help and listen carefully to emergency instructions.

These suggestions are very brief and don't list all of the emergencies you may face. Ask your doctor ahead of time for more information on ways to be prepared for baby's emergencies.

First Step: Call for help immediately! (See page 98.)

Additional Steps

Choking	• Straighten baby's back. Turn baby over on your lap and slap baby sharply on the back. • Clear baby's mouth with your finger. **Be careful not to push object further in.** • Give mouth to mouth resuscitation, if you have been trained to do it. • Follow instructions from the emergency medical staff that you call.
Poisoning	• With bottle or item **and baby** in hand, call the Poison Control Center, 911 or emergency room at hospital. • Do not use Syrup of Ipecac® unless told to do so by the medical professional.
Burns	• Immediately run or pour **cold water on the burned area.** • Take off clothes on the burned area if they are not stuck to the wound. • **If skin is off a large area, the burn needs to be seen by a doctor.**
Falls	• Check baby from head to toe for obvious broken bones. If your child is old enough, ask him to move the area that hurts. **Watch your child closely after the injury.** If baby seems overly tired, looks exceptionally pale, dizzy or is vomiting call your doctor. • If there are no signs of serious injury, apply a cold pack to the tender area, but stay close to baby and keep checking for symptoms.
Bleeding wounds	• Apply pressure on wound with clean cloth for **three or four minutes.** If you let up too soon, the wound may continue to bleed. • Clean area with soap and water. • Wide, gaping wounds or wounds with jagged edges may need stitches. • Follow doctor's instructions for further care.

Emergency Numbers

Keep these numbers handy for everyone in your home who may need to call for help—grandparents, babysitters, friends. If you don't have a phone in your home, keep a set of the numbers in your wallet or purse so you have them when you need them. Baby's diaper bag is another good place to have emergency phone numbers. Keep change on hand for pay phones, too.

911 Direct line for all emergencies. (You don't need money to call 911 from a pay phone.)

Police: _____

Fire: _____

Emergency Room/Hospital:

_____

_____

Poison Control Center: _____

_____

Doctor: _____

_____

_____

Others to Call for Help:

_____

_____

_____

_____

_____

_____

_____

Pharmacist: _____

_____

Taxi: _____

_____

_____

School: _____

_____

_____

Work: _____

_____

_____

Child Care: _____

_____

Second Choice Child Care:

_____

_____

Others important numbers:

_____

_____

_____

_____

_____

_____

_____

_____

_____

_____

_____

_____

Safe Family: A Personal Plan

Taking time to look around you and think about a safety plan of action for your home and family is an important step toward keeping your baby safe. One way to begin is to read over the information on the previous pages. Next, think about your child's age and abilities— both now and in the near future. (For more about child development, see Chapter 7.) Then, do a child's-eye tour of your home. You may want to get down on your hands and knees and crawl room by room, checking out the floor, furniture, toys, electrical outlets, and more. What are some emergency preparations or plans you might want to make? Finally, write down what you discover and the steps needed to make your home safest for baby.

As you watch your baby grow and change, you may soon realize that you need to adapt your personal family safety plan to stay ahead of baby's new abilities and skills.

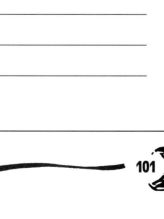

Your Notes

You can use this page to make notes about things you've learned, questions you have, milestones reached, and more. It can be a record of some of the events in your life as a new parent—your dreams, memories, concerns, hopes, and plans. Or perhaps this is a place to write down and celebrate baby's changes, growth and development —that first tooth, first word, first step...

Chapter 7
Your Growing Child

Babies grow and change at an amazing rate! Every day seems to bring a new accomplishment. This chapter offers information about all the wonderful ways your baby is growing, what baby can do at each age and how to help your child grow strong, healthy and smart. There are ideas on helping your child through some big steps, like toilet training. The guidance and discipline section has suggestions for getting off to the right start by encouraging behavior that helps baby get along in her world.

What Every Baby Needs

Your baby is growing at a very fast pace. You will see more changes—physical, intellectual and emotional—during the first two years than at any other time in your child's life. This development is "programmed" into every child. Kids develop in basically the same way. They learn to walk, talk, and express their feelings in an orderly pattern. What is different about each child is the pace or rate at which she develops. Some children will quickly learn to walk or talk; others may do it more slowly. There is a wide range of normal development. A child will grow and change on his own, but parents can enrich his life—give him the "fertilizer"—so that he will grow even stronger and more completely. It's up to parents to help their children grow and develop in many ways.

All children need these things to grow strong and healthy both physically and emotionally.

Love

Babies need tons of undiluted, pure, unconditional love. This means loving baby for who he is and all he can or can't do. It means not wishing he was someone else, that he behaved differently, that he was different in some other way. It means loving him when he is being "difficult" and when he is being "easy," when he is awake and when he is asleep. It means sharing him with the wider world, too, so grandparents, cousins, siblings, friends and others can love him, too. No baby can be loved too much.

Basic care

Kids need healthy food, plenty of sleep, clean, warm clothes, shoes that fit, a safe place to live and play, visits to the doctor (both when they are sick and for immunizations and well-baby checks), regular baths and all the other things that go into maintaining life. Without these things a child will not grow and develop to the best of his ability.

Understanding

A baby needs parents who understand her. Understanding parents know about child development and watch their child as she develops so they know what stage of growth she is in. They use this information to have realistic expectations of what she can do and to help her learn and grow. Understanding parents help baby start to grow independent and do things for herself, while being there for her when she needs them.

Stimulation

This means doing a variety of interesting things with baby to encourage body and brain development. Researchers have learned that during the first three years of life important, physical connections are made in baby's brains. These connections are what make it possible for baby to continue learning throughout her life, to develop into a strong person who believes in herself and cares about others. Parents can help stimulate baby's body and brain to grow and develop. They can play with baby, let her explore and try new things and they can encourage independence by offering her space and time to try things on her own.

Play

Play is a child's work. It's her job to play. As she plays, she is learning how things work, how people get along, what to do to solve a problem, how to use her imagination, and many more things that will help her learn and grow. Play is fun, but it's also learning and development. Parents can help their child have plenty of chances to play in many different ways.

(continued)

What Every Baby Needs *(continued)*

Shared Parenting

It's not required but babies can benefit from having parents who believe in the benefits of shared parenting. Moms and dads who are committed to raising their child—whether in the same home or in different ones—can give their child the love and attention of the two people who care the most about baby and who will work together to help him develop to the best of his ability. See pages 7-12 for more about shared parenting.

Communication

Talking and listening are two of the most important things parents do with their children. Talking to baby helps her learn to talk and listening to her encourages her to talk and to express her feelings. Both are important to her development.

Routines

Baby grows best when she knows what will happen. It helps her make sense of the world when she knows that there is a time for each activity of her day—eating, sleeping, bathing, playing, going to day care, coming home. Parents make the first routines for young children and then change them as baby grows and wants a say in how the routine works.

Guidance and Discipline

Loving guidance and discipline helps a child get along in the world. Understanding the expectations of home and other places protects children and helps them get along in different situations. Parents help baby by showing and teaching him the rules of behavior and reinforcing the rules in ways he understands. Children need and want limits and boundaries in their lives. A child without limits may feel unsure and insecure. Without limits, he doesn't know what is expected of him, doesn't know how to behave in different situations, and can't set limits for himself.

Safety and security

All children need a safe place to live and play. A home that is childproofed encourages exploration and play, which are key parts of development. Parents must protect baby from the real dangers of the world and give him the tools and skills he needs to handle the dangers he may face on his own as he grows.

Beyond physical safety, a child needs to feel secure, too. He needs to know that his parents love him and care about him and his needs. He needs to know that no matter how far he may wander, actually or in terms of his behavior, he is still loved and valued by his parents. A child who has this sense of love and security is able to go off on his own to test his abilities because he knows someone loves him and will help him when he needs it.

Ways Baby Changes

As baby grows and changes, so will her daily activities and routines. Parents must adapt how they care for baby as she changes. She may eat less but will eat different things. Her sleep patterns will change as she is awake for longer periods of time. Diaper changes may be less frequent but bowel movements may be on a regular schedule. Her temperament will become more apparent as her moods settle. She will learn to play in different ways and will start to show a preference for certain toys. All of these changes are exciting for parents and baby. Encourage baby as she tries new things.

	Birth to Three Months	Three to Six Months	Six to Nine Months	Nine Months to Two Years
Eating	Hunger is so strong, it almost hurts. Baby literally cannot wait to eat. Takes milk feedings only, every two to five hours.	Can wait a few minutes before feeding. Eats every three to five hours. Takes milk feedings only.	Starts to eat three daily meals with solid food, plus two milk-only meals.	Eats three meals a day, plus three snacks. Can go from baby food to regular table food.
Sleeping	Sleeps most of the time when not eating—about 16 to 18 hours a day. Sleep unsettled, yet baby can sleep through noise.	Sleep 10 to 12 hours at night with usually three naps a day. Sleep is quieter. Awake for longer periods.	Sleeps 10 to 12 hours at night and takes two naps. Baby can be awakened by noise. May have some sleep problems at eight to 12 months.	Sleeps 10 to 12 hours at night. Toddlers start to move toward one nap a day.

(continued)

Ways Baby Changes *(continued)*

	Birth to Three Months	Three to Six Months	Six to Nine Months	Nine Months to Two Years
Bladder/ bowel control	Has diapers which are both wet and soiled 6 to 10 times a day. Bowel movements runny, unformed, light colored.	Fewer wet diapers. Sometimes wet without bowel movement. Bowel movement is firmer, brown.	Wets four to six times a day. Usually bowel movement at certain time of day. May have diarrhea due to teething or some new foods.	Can stay dry and unsoiled for longer periods but not yet ready for toilet training.
Play	Attention span for play about five minutes.	May spend 10 to 15 minutes at a time playing with a toy.	Starts to move around to get to what she wants to play with. May entertain self (with parent in room) for 15 to 20 minutes.	**9 to 18 months** May play independently for up to 15 to 20 minutes. Parents need to be in same room to help and play now and then. This age likes to practice climbing, crawling and other physical skills. **18 to 24 months** Starts playing near, but not with, other children. Likes physical play and exploration. Attention to independent play is longer now, too.

Child Development: What and When

Understanding how baby grows and changes is important. Parents who know what to expect at different ages are able to provide encouragement and support focused on that stage of development. They can help baby through the tough stages—the terrible twos, for example—with love and understanding. They understand that this is "just a phase"—an important phase—in development. Parents who know child development don't expect baby to do things she's not yet able to do. They understand that some kids can walk at ten months and don't talk until 18 months. Or vice versa. They know and love baby for who and what he is and work with him to help him grow into all he can be.

There are many, many sources of detailed information on child development. This is a very short summary of some of the high points of development. Keep in mind that these developmental milestones happen over a wider range of ages than we have listed here. If you're worried or have questions about development, talk to your doctor.

3 months

Looks at parents and watches faces.

Startles at loud noises.

Raises head when lying on stomach.

Cries when hungry or uncomfortable.

Smiles, laughs.

Coos or gurgles.

Follows movement by turning head.

Reaches for a toy.

Holds hands together.

Can grasp a rattle or other similar plaything.

6 months

May be teething.

Rolls over well.

Holds head up without support.

May be able to sit independently.

Reaches for and holds onto objects.

Passes toy from one hand to the other.

Tries to put everything in mouth.

Can feed himself a cracker—but is messy.

Works to get a toy that's out of reach.

Turns towards sounds.

Babbles or tries to imitate speech.

Laughs out loud.

9 months

Picks up a small object, like a Cheerio®, with two fingers.

Crawls.

Knows own name.

Cries when parent leaves.

May say dada or mama.

Imitates sounds.

Stands but needs to hold onto something.

Bangs two toys or other things together.

Plays peek-a-boo and pat-a-cake.

Waves bye-bye.

Can eat finger foods.

1 Year

Says "no" but means many things.

Stands alone.

Starts to walk.

Says a few words besides mama and dada.

Drinks from a cup.

Rolls ball back to parent.

Starts to let parent know what she wants without crying.

(continued)

Child Development: What and When *(continued)*

18 months

Tries to put on own shoes or other clothes.

Can use a spoon.

Likes to help.

Points to some things when asked to.

Walks without help.

Builds tower with two to four blocks.

Can kick a ball.

Combines two different words.

Can scribble with pencil or crayon.

Puts things into other things—shape sorters, puzzles.

Starts to sort things.

Can follow simple directions—bring requested toy.

2 Years

Listens to short stories.

Turns pages of book.

Copies another child's play.

Jumps in place.

Walks up and down stairs with help.

May do the opposite of what's asked or expected.

Starts to name some feelings.

Can wash and dry hands with some help.

Names pictures in a book.

Follows directions better.

Can draw lines.

Can pour to empty containers.

Throws ball overhand.

3 years

May be ready for toilet training.

Talks and is usually understood.

Can tell you his first and last name.

Uses three-word sentences.

Knows and can say who is a boy or a girl.

Learning to recognize and name colors.

Peddles a trike.

Runs with few falls.

Imitates drawing.

Can string large objects.

Can name six body parts.

Holds fork with a fist.

Starts to prefer one hand over the other.

Is starting to be ready for three-step directions.

Parents and Babies: What's Different

Babies are not little adults. They are unique individuals whose eating, playing, growth and development are very different from that of grown-ups. It's important to realize that parents and babies are very different in their needs and abilities. Parents can't make decisions for baby based on their own needs or wants. Parents must understand what baby needs and can do. Here are some ways parents and babies are different.

 Babies

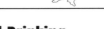 **Parents**

Eating and Drinking

	Babies	Parents
Parents and babies need different diets.	An infant's digestive system is very sensitive. Either breast milk or formula is all an infant needs. At around six months, baby can start certain solid foods. It's unnecessary to add salt, spices or sugar to baby's solid food.	Parents could never live on liquid alone. Most can eat just about anything—you've heard of people with "cast iron stomachs!" Parents need a variety of foods to meet nutritional needs and use salt, spices and sugar to enhance their food.
Hunger is more urgent in babies	Hunger is physically painful to babies three or four months old or younger. When baby needs to eat she needs to eat NOW. Hunger can make babies and toddlers very unhappy, frustrated or irritable.	Parents can often put off eating, at least for awhile. Hunger can make parents irritable and less energetic, but it usually isn't physically painful, nor does it stop them completely.

Physical Growth & Development

	Babies	Parents
Physical Coordination Differs	Newborns aren't born with eye-hand coordination or other small motor skills yet. She can't easily do things like put a rattle in her mouth or pick up a pea with her fingers. Baby will develop these skills and much more as she grows.	Parents have different levels of eye-hand coordination and small motor skills. Some are very adept at sports such as basketball or tennis. Others are good at putting stuff together or have nice handwriting. It can be easy to forget that we had to learn these skills as our muscles developed.

(continued)

Babies

Parents

Physical Growth & Development
(continued)

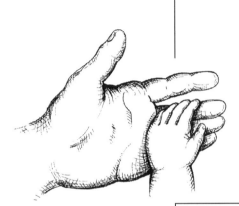

Sleep needs

Babies vary in their need for sleep. Baby needs a lot of sleep because she is growing and changing very fast. In general newborns sleep between feedings, usually in stretches of two to three hours. By about age one, baby may be down to two naps a day. By 24 months old, he may be down to one nap a day.

Parents' sleep needs vary from person to person, too. Some need at least 8 or more hours of sleep a night to function, while others may need less. Those who are parents, however, probably need a lot of sleep to keep up with the changes and activities of a new baby. Breastfeeding mothers especially need sleep due to demands on their bodies.

Thinking, Feeling and Learning

Babies don't see another's point of view

Baby is very self-centered. He must be because his whole existence depends upon making sure his needs are known. Baby thinks the world is there for him and his needs. Not until a baby is age three or older will he begin to understand that other people have feelings, too.

Parents do understand that others have feelings, too. They can make decisions which consider others' feelings. Parents try to make their decisions based on what is best for their baby because they can see the world from baby's eyes.

Behavior Differences

Babies have to use behavior to get attention because they can't talk. They cry to say their gums hurt from teething or they're wet or have a tummy ache. Babies don't cry to upset parents or to get their way. They cry because they need something.

Parents can use words to ask for attention or to get what they need. They don't have to use behavior alone to get what they want.

(continued)

111

Babies

Parents

Thinking, Feeling and Learning
(continued)

	Babies	Parents
Self-Control	Baby cannot control her actions or feelings. She can't be quiet "on demand" or not touch something when she is told not to touch. She will react in her most natural way according to her surroundings. She reacts this way not to either please or upset her parents, but because that is her natural reaction. A child must be age three or older before she can begin to control her actions and reactions.	Parents can make decisions about their behavior. They can choose to do something or not do something. Parents can control their feelings such as anger, too. Adults can understand that babies aren't in control of their feelings or actions; parents then help baby be more in control.
Emotions	Baby has no idea what emotions like mad, angry, loving or jealous are or how these emotions feel. She can't even think those thoughts. She cries because she's uncomfortable or afraid. She smiles because shes's proud or feels good or because someone smiles back.	Parents can usually tell when they are feeling a certain emotion. They may cry when sad, but know why they're crying and can use words to express those feelings, too. Parents communicate their feelings in many ways. They don't have to cry or smile to say it all.
Routines	Baby thrives on routines and predictability in the daily things of life. Having a routine for bedtime, for example, makes it easier for baby to sleep because he knows what to expect. Baby learns by experiencing things over and over. He learns about the whole world by learning about one small part.	Variety is the spice of life for many grown-ups. Parents enjoy doing and learning through new experiences. Routines might seem boring, but adults can benefit from following some routines, too.

Your Baby's Temperament

Temperament, sometimes called personality, is how a baby or parent responds to and interacts with the world.

No one is all one type of temperament. We all have a combination of characteristics—some more evident that others.

Parents can learn more about baby's temperament by looking at the following nine characteristics. From these, three temperament types become clear—quiet, moderate, active. Parents often find it helpful and interesting to learn about baby's personal style and ways of reacting to their world.

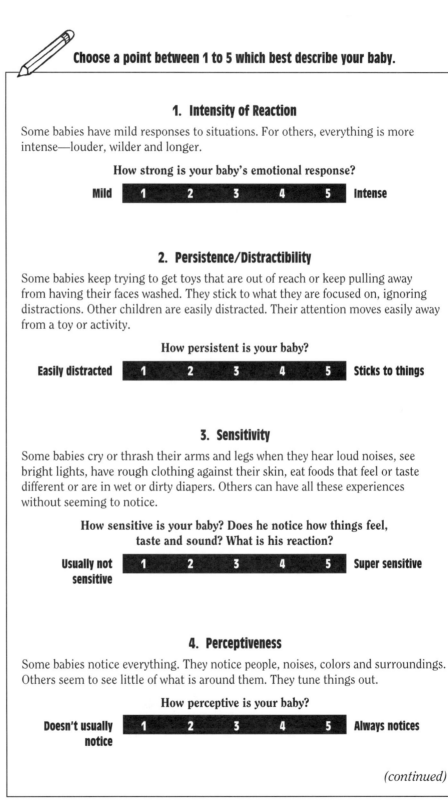

Choose a point between 1 to 5 which best describe your baby.

1. Intensity of Reaction

Some babies have mild responses to situations. For others, everything is more intense—louder, wilder and longer.

How strong is your baby's emotional response?

Mild | 1   2   3   4   5 | Intense

2. Persistence/Distractibility

Some babies keep trying to get toys that are out of reach or keep pulling away from having their faces washed. They stick to what they are focused on, ignoring distractions. Other children are easily distracted. Their attention moves easily away from a toy or activity.

How persistent is your baby?

Easily distracted | 1   2   3   4   5 | Sticks to things

3. Sensitivity

Some babies cry or thrash their arms and legs when they hear loud noises, see bright lights, have rough clothing against their skin, eat foods that feel or taste different or are in wet or dirty diapers. Others can have all these experiences without seeming to notice.

How sensitive is your baby? Does he notice how things feel, taste and sound? What is his reaction?

Usually not sensitive | 1   2   3   4   5 | Super sensitive

4. Perceptiveness

Some babies notice everything. They notice people, noises, colors and surroundings. Others seem to see little of what is around them. They tune things out.

How perceptive is your baby?

Doesn't usually notice | 1   2   3   4   5 | Always notices

(continued)

Your Baby's Temperament *(continued)*

Parents and children can sometimes have very different temperaments. This can offer interesting challenges. How does your temperament compare to your child's?

You can look at your temperament using this same scale. Look at the descriptions and instead of "your baby" ask how you are or how you react in certain similar situations.

If it seems your temperament is very different from your baby's, spend some time thinking how this might affect the ways you respond and understand baby. Remember, if you think something needs to change in the way you interact with baby, it's up to you. Baby can't change.

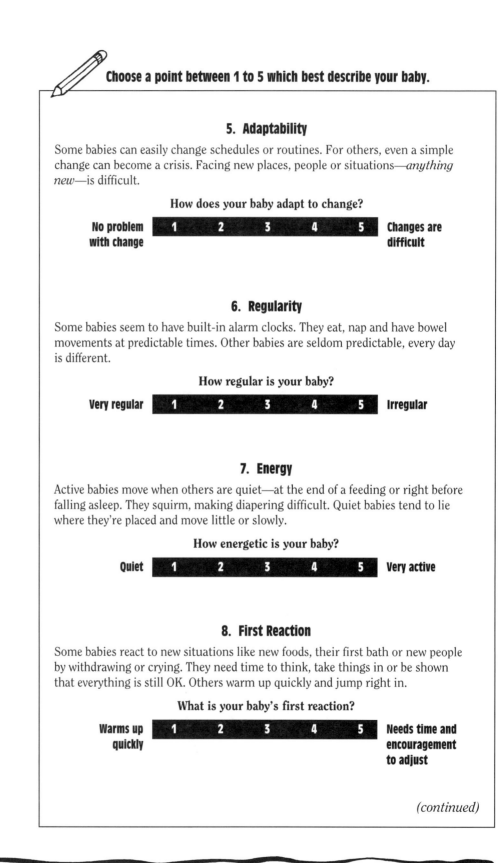

Choose a point between 1 to 5 which best describe your baby.

5. Adaptability

Some babies can easily change schedules or routines. For others, even a simple change can become a crisis. Facing new places, people or situations—*anything new*—is difficult.

How does your baby adapt to change?

No problem with change | 1 2 3 4 5 | Changes are difficult

6. Regularity

Some babies seem to have built-in alarm clocks. They eat, nap and have bowel movements at predictable times. Other babies are seldom predictable, every day is different.

How regular is your baby?

Very regular | 1 2 3 4 5 | Irregular

7. Energy

Active babies move when others are quiet—at the end of a feeding or right before falling asleep. They squirm, making diapering difficult. Quiet babies tend to lie where they're placed and move little or slowly.

How energetic is your baby?

Quiet | 1 2 3 4 5 | Very active

8. First Reaction

Some babies react to new situations like new foods, their first bath or new people by withdrawing or crying. They need time to think, take things in or be shown that everything is still OK. Others warm up quickly and jump right in.

What is your baby's first reaction?

Warms up quickly | 1 2 3 4 5 | Needs time and encouragement to adjust

(continued)

Your Baby's Temperament *(continued)*

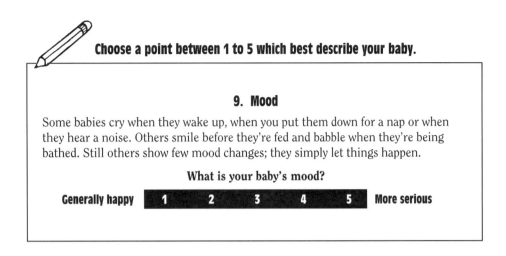

Choose a point between 1 to 5 which best describe your baby.

9. Mood

Some babies cry when they wake up, when you put them down for a nap or when they hear a noise. Others smile before they're fed and babble when they're being bathed. Still others show few mood changes; they simply let things happen.

What is your baby's mood?

Generally happy | 1 | 2 | 3 | 4 | 5 | More serious

To determine your child's temperament:

Look over your responses. Total your answers and mark the total on the scale below.

9	27	45
Quiet	Moderate	Active

Quiet
This baby tends to be quiet and docile. When faced with new or changing situations, he will be more inclined to withdraw than to react intensely.

Moderate
This baby tends to have a more regular schedule for when she naps, eats and has bowel movements. She may adapt more easily to new situations, is easygoing and has a generally more unruffled outlook.

Active
Active refers not only to the level of physical activity but also to the depth of his response, his general mood, less rhythm in his schedule for sleep, etc. and strong reactions to strangers and to changes.

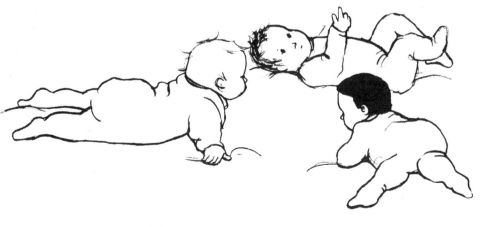

A Sense of Self

Children do best when they are helped to develop a strong, positive sense of self: self-awareness, self-confidence, self-esteem. This helps children get along in the world because it gives them important skills that aids them in bouncing back from problems, understanding feelings and reactions (their own and others), developing friendships, standing up for what they believe, and so much more. The development of a sense of self begins at birth and parents can encourage a strong, positive outcome in many ways.

Love and affection

Let your baby know how much you love her. Respond to her cries, try to soothe her. Hold her close to your body, make eye contact, talk, sing and laugh with baby. Teach her about ways to behave with a gentle manner. Let your child know you cherish her. A grin or a kiss from across the room when a toddler does something good, helps her feel worthwhile and loved.

Accept feelings

When your child turns to you scared by a loud noise, you might say, "That was a big boom. It's scary, isn't it?" Let her know you understand and care.

Learn about baby

Every child is special and unique. Save a few minutes each day to just sit quietly and watch baby in action. You may be amazed at what you discover about her personality and abilities. Learn as much as you can about child development and temperament so you know what to expect next and ways baby may respond to his changing world.

Avoid surprises

Try not to spring surprises on baby. Stick to your routines. This helps your child feel that her world is safe, predictable and not overwhelming. But, some changes and surprises are just a part of life. When they do occur and if baby gets upset, help him settle down again. Tell him that he is OK, that you're there for him and that he can adjust. Use a calm, gentle voice.

Focus on baby

Give your baby focused attention. It's important to let baby know that he has "all of you." If your child wants your attention when you can't give it, be honest. But make sure you spend some focused time with your baby every day.

Be respectful

Treat your child with respect and kindness. Ask yourself, "Would I talk to or treat my friends the same way I talk to or treat my child?"

Adapt to baby

Keep in mind that babies are not here to please and serve parents. Stay flexible so your can adapt your agenda to meet baby's needs; don't expect him to adjust to your schedule, needs or plans.

Learn abilities

Understand your child's abilities. If he can cooperate for only 20 minutes in a store, don't plan a two-hour shopping trip—especially at naptime. Let your child's unique qualities unfold gradually and celebrate their development.

Your baby's role model—take care of yourself, too!

- Have something on your mind? Find positive ways to express yourself. Have someone in your life that you can trust to listen and give you helpful feedback.

- Take care of your body. Get enough sleep, eat healthy foods, exercise, and more.

- Having a rough day? List the good things about you and your child. Don't lose sight of all the special stuff that makes you so important to each other.

- Don't ever forget—you must be a wonderful, special person because someone important loves you very much. Your baby!

Helping Kids Feel Secure

Another part of giving children strong self-esteem is to let them know that they are safe and loved. This feeling of security begins when they are infants as their mom or dad lovingly respond to their needs. When parents continue to create a home for baby that is filled with love, trust and physical safety, baby can grow, learn and become more independent. He is confident that his parents love him, are there for him and will keep him safe.

Know Your Baby

- A child's feelings of security and safety begin in infancy. It's based on the long-lasting emotional bond that develops between newborns and parents. Experts call this "security of attachment." The bond grows and develops over time as parents care for respond to baby's need for food, love, dry diapers, attention and more.

- Security of attachment is important. The child with a secure attachment has many of these characteristics:

  – A baby with secure attachment is able to try out all his abilities to the fullest. He knows you are there when needed to help or guide. This child feels safe enough to explore on his own. He knows that even if he has annoyed dad or mom, they still love him.

  – An older child with secure attachments has a confident, eager attitude as she explores her world. She tends to be friendly and others are attracted to her. In addition, she has high self-esteem, greater self-reliance and more flexibility in how she responds to her world.

- The confident, secure child is protected in many ways.

  – He understands that there are limits to behavior, his and others, which helps him adjust to different situations.

  – She knows reliable, caring adults can be turned to for help when needed.

  – He can do some things for himself and is eager to try more.

  – She can meet the challenges of different or new situations.

Know Yourself

- For a child to feel secure, he needs to know his parents will "be there" him—by being physically and emotionally close to him.

- Throughout baby's development, warmth, nurturing and respect for baby's needs and point of view are important characteristics for parents. These are part of being emotionally available to the child.

- Reliability leads to trust. A parent needs to be consistent so that a child knows he can depend on his parent in any and every situation.

- Parents can develop a style that promotes self-reliance and flexibility in children. Parents can gradually give a child more independence, while being available to help when baby needs it.

Know the Situation

- Parents may worry that baby's attachment to them may be affected if parents need to leave baby in a child care setting while they work or go to school. Research shows that children can develop attachments to more than one caregiver. As long as parents remain emotionally and physically available to baby, other healthy attachments will form just fine.

- Security of attachment can be hurt by stress in a family, unhappy adult relationships and the lack of supportive help for parents.

- Parents may not be able to control the details of a stressful situation, but they can control how they react to it, deal with it, and explain it to their children. How they do these things will affect a child's feeling of security and safety.

Giving Baby's Brain a Boost

Parents hear a lot about stimulation and brain development these days. Researchers have found that the first few years of life are vital to a child's long-term ability to learn. In these first years, connections in the brain develop so that it's "wired" to learn all that children need to learn. Parents help make these connections when they do the things that many parents do naturally—talk, sing, coo and play with baby. Here are some ways to give your baby's brain a boost.

Love That Baby

A baby that develops a loving attachment to her parents feels loved and safe. She gets these feelings when her world is predicable and she knows her needs will be met. She knows when she cries, mom or dad will be there with food, a dry diaper, a warm blanket, a soothing pat or a hug and a kiss. A securely attached baby becomes more self-confident, curious and better able to adjust to new situations. These skills help her to explore and learn. Consistent and responsive care promotes brain development. There is nothing more important to your child's development and learning, than the love you show your child.

Stimulation

Stimulation is a big word that means giving baby interesting, fun things to do and try. In the beginning, this means you. Baby loves parents' faces and voices. Give baby your time and attention each day. You can sing, play, read books, laugh, pretend, dance and cuddle. Look into her eyes and tell her how important she is and how much you love her. A safe and interesting environment helps create the wiring in a baby's brain. As she grows, show her how to do things and play with her. Then stand back and watch how she learns. You will be able to see her growing and learning every day.

Early Learning— Right From the Start

The first three years seem to be the time when the brain is most able to develop the important connections it needs to learn. These years are the best times to learn about language, to develop large and small muscles, to learn about feelings, their's and others', and how the world fits together. If important brain development is missed during the infant and toddler years, there are ways to make up for it later, but missing these windows of opportunity can make it harder for baby to learn later. So, don't miss out. Offer a variety of leaning opportunities right from the start.

Healthy Babies Learn Best

Babies don't drink, smoke, do drugs or eat junk food. Poor nutrition, secondhand smoke and chemical abuse by those around him impacts a child's brain development, too. Don't risk his potential by polluting his environment. Critical steps in healthy development include regular health care visits, immunizations, good family nutrition, and a child safe environment. Keep your family free of violence and drug and alcohol abuse. Baby will be better off and so will you.

Taking Care of the Expert—You!

Take advantage of information that gives you and your child a head start. Try out parent education classes, join a support group, check out books and videos from the library. Talk to other parents about being a parent. Keep yourself healthy and chemical free. Live safely. Remember, your child depends on you. Take care of yourself.

118

Just Playing?

How a baby plays will change as she grows. What she is learning changes, too. She keeps building on what she's learned before every time she plays. Babies begin by playing and reacting to parents and others. One-year-olds continue to want to play with parents, but start doing some things on their own. Toddlers and preschoolers can do more and more.

Skills That Develop As Baby Plays

Skills	Play That Helps Develop Skills
Problem-solving	• Tries to get to an out-of-reach toy. • Shakes rattle to make noise. • Builds with blocks, boxes and more. • Learns to make things move, turn, open, etc. • Untangles something, fits pieces together, gets clothes on. • Matches colors or shapes in puzzles or games.
Social abilities	• Talks back when parent "talks." • Makes faces in mirror. • Talks or babbles about the things around them. Listens when another talks. • Finds ways to play, take turns and cooperate with another.
Imagination	• Imitates what parent does—waves arms, makes face… • Responds to music and songs. • Acts out parts of their daily lives—makes dinner, reads the newspaper, rides on the bus. • Works through problems by acting them out—maybe a teddy bear gets comforted about a scary situation or gets scolded for a "no-no." • Makes up stories, songs, rhymes. • Includes others in their "let's pretend" play. • Uses props in imaginative play (toy phone, toy car, baby doll, etc.).
Feelings	• Recognizes parents' feelings by noticing changes in facial expressions, tone of voice and more. • Tells another child or adult her feelings—uses words and/or body language. • Recognizes others' feelings—"She's sad, her mom left." • Acts out discipline situations, for example, gives a doll a time-out. • Comforts others—children, adults, dolls, pets. • Takes care of dolls and stuffed animals—feeding, clothing, comforting and more.

(continued)

Just Playing? *(continued)*

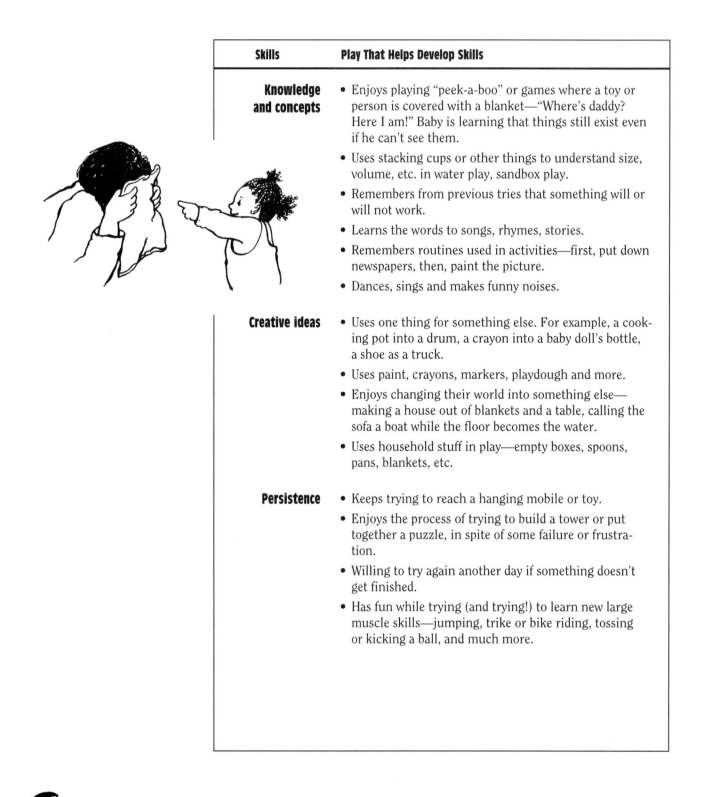

Skills	Play That Helps Develop Skills
Knowledge and concepts	• Enjoys playing "peek-a-boo" or games where a toy or person is covered with a blanket—"Where's daddy? Here I am!" Baby is learning that things still exist even if he can't see them.
	• Uses stacking cups or other things to understand size, volume, etc. in water play, sandbox play.
	• Remembers from previous tries that something will or will not work.
	• Learns the words to songs, rhymes, stories.
	• Remembers routines used in activities—first, put down newspapers, then, paint the picture.
	• Dances, sings and makes funny noises.
Creative ideas	• Uses one thing for something else. For example, a cooking pot into a drum, a crayon into a baby doll's bottle, a shoe as a truck.
	• Uses paint, crayons, markers, playdough and more.
	• Enjoys changing their world into something else—making a house out of blankets and a table, calling the sofa a boat while the floor becomes the water.
	• Uses household stuff in play—empty boxes, spoons, pans, blankets, etc.
Persistence	• Keeps trying to reach a hanging mobile or toy.
	• Enjoys the process of trying to build a tower or put together a puzzle, in spite of some failure or frustration.
	• Willing to try again another day if something doesn't get finished.
	• Has fun while trying (and trying!) to learn new large muscle skills—jumping, trike or bike riding, tossing or kicking a ball, and much more.

Playing With Your Baby

Playing with baby is one of the delights of parenthood. Parents can spend hours entertaining and interacting with baby. And guess what? This is a great way to help baby grow strong muscles, intelligence, self-esteem and imagination. When parents care for and play with baby, they are also increasing the love and attachment between them.

Play Ideas—Birth to Six Months Old

Growing Strong	Learning to Play	Learning to Talk	Becoming a Person
Play roly-poly by gently rolling baby from tummy to back.	Make faces at baby—smile, frown, laugh, wrinkle your nose.	Comfort baby when he cries.	Play peek-a-boo. Baby learns you come back, even when you "disappear."
Give baby a gentle horsey ride on your foot. Sing while you bounce him.	Gently rub noses and kiss his fingers, feet, toes.	Make noises—whisper, giggle, whistle, hum, and talk, talk, talk.	Hold baby in front of mirror and talk about what you can see.
Gently move baby's arms and legs. Touch her hands and fingers, feet and toes. Loving touch helps baby learn what is part of her body and what is not.	Catch baby's attention with something bright. Move it slowly in different directions for baby to follow it with her eyes.	Sing songs, say rhymes. Read picture books with simple words and bright pictures.	Name body parts while pointing to the parts. Tell baby how wonderful he looks—his eyes, the color of his skin, the texture of his hair, his lovely toes.
Roll a ball a few feet from baby and encourage her to crawl toward it.	Play simple finger games—This Little Pig or Pat-a-Cake. Pass a rattle back and forth between you and baby. Say, "Here you are," and "Thank you."	Take turns "talking" with baby—talk and let her respond. Imitate her sounds. Make toys and animals talk to baby. Encourage her to talk back.	Let baby set the pace when meeting someone new. Give baby the security of routines, especially at bedtime.
Stand baby on your lap and let him bounce up and down.	Let baby sit where he can see things that move—shadows, sunlight, mobiles.	Let him hear different sounds—barking dogs, ringing bells, cars.	Cover baby's face with blanket. Act surprised when he pulls it off and reappears.
Let baby use your body as a hill to climb.	Float some brightly colored balls in baby's bath. She will try to catch them. Use a baby-safe mirror to show baby his smiles and other expressions.		Childproof so baby can play without too many limits.

(continued)

121

Playing With Your Baby *(continued)*

Play Ideas—6 to 12 Months Old

Growing Strong	Learning to Play	Learning to Talk	Becoming a Person
Set up a simple obstacle course for a new crawler—one small pillow to crawl over or around. Add more as he can do more. Put a toy just out of reach and encourage baby to crawl after it. Carefully hold baby while you both slowly ride back and forth on a swing. If baby gets scared, quit and try again when baby is older. Put toys on the seat of a couch and help baby pull herself up to reach them. Take turns tossing or dropping bean bags in a box. Here is a fast and easy "bean bag" to make: take a clean sock, add some dried rice or cereal (nothing bigger), tie a very tight knot in the sock. Have a cupboard just for baby. Fill it with plastic cups, wooden spoons, pots.	Encourage baby to pick up small pieces of bread or cereal with finger and thumb. Baby will like playing and painting with yogurt or spaghetti on his highchair tray. Stick strips of masking tape on highchair tray for baby to pull off and re-stick. Blow soap bubbles for baby to watch float away. Make a sorting toy by cutting a large and small hole in the plastic lid of a coffee can. Let baby try to fit different sized things through the holes. (Make sure the objects to fit into the holes are baby safe.)	Talk to your baby and listen when she talks back. Look at and read books with your baby. Sing to and with your baby. Let baby drop blocks or small balls into a large can to hear different sounds. Make rhythm instruments out of boxes or pans and wooden spoons	Respond to baby so he knows you notice what he is trying to tell you. Make baby laugh by doing silly things like putting her hat on your head or pretend to drink from her bottle. Hide a toy under a blanket and ask baby, "Where is the toy?" Act surprised when baby finds it. Let baby get finger foods out of small containers. Roll a ball back and forth between you. Play follow the leader. Do simple actions like clapping hands and ask baby to do it, too. Keep childproofing so she can explore freely.

(continued)

Playing With Your Baby *(continued)*

Play Ideas—1 to 3 Years Old

Growing Strong	Learning to Play	Learning to Talk	Becoming a Person
Make tunnels to crawl through with a table and blanket or big boxes. Find wide open spaces for running and climbing. Play catch with a bean bag. Take a wagon along on walks. Let him pull it. Make an obstacle course with pillows, pots to walk on, furniture to crawl over. Blow bubbles for child to chase. Set up a landing pad with pillows for child to jump down on. Dance to different types of music.	Have different containers to fill with sand and dump. Show him how to make different types of lines and shapes. Play with play-dough using cookie cutters and simple tools. Encourage eating with a spoon and fork. Let him feed his baby doll. Sort things into groups—all spoons, all square blocks, all blue cars.	Play listening games. Sit close and say, "Shhh, can you hear (a baby crying, a bird singing, a bell ringing.)" Play word games. Rhyming is fun. Puppets have interesting conversations. Listen and talk to your child. Sing together. Introduce to baby different kinds of music. Teach baby to make different animal sounds, car noises and more.	Be sure childproofing is enough to let child explore freely. Playing near other kids helps her learn to get along. Simple rules of getting along can be explained. Let toddlers help with chores.

Toys and Kids

There are so many playthings available, it can be hard to figure out which ones are good and have a lot of play value. Keep in mind that the best toys don't necessarily come from a store. Look around to see what you might already have for baby to safely play with. Keep in mind that for baby, you are the most fun, important and interesting plaything in the world!

This list of playthings has suggestions for those that can encourage different areas of development. The age ranges are approximate and many toys for younger babies are also great for older children.

Be sure to check out **Toy Safety for Little Ones** on pages 90-91.

Intellectual Development	Emotional Development	Physical Development	
		Large Muscles	Small Muscles
Birth to 6 Months Old			
• Stuffed animals • Baby-safe (plastic) mirror • Toys that make noises—chimes, rattles, squeaks	• Puppets/dolls • Pop-up toys • Sturdy books	• Soft balls/blocks • Toys with different textures or movements • Crib mobile • Teethers	• Bouncer chairs • Push toys • Balls
6 to 12 Months Old			
• Toy phone • Simple problem-solving toys (for example, push a button and something pops up) • Simple picture books • Music	• Child-size "adult" items—spoon, cup, purse, tools • Dolls, soft toys	• Fat crayons • Purses • Bucket with lid • Blocks • Trucks/cars • Nesting/stacking toys	• Push toys—toy grocery cart, strollers • Balls of all sizes • Bean bags • Stuff to crawl over
1 to 3 Years Old			
• Simple props for play—cups, dishes, hats, phone • Realistic toys like parents' tools, doctor kit • Books, books, books	• Toy people, cars, animals • Things to share—blocks, boxes of crayons • Dress-up stuff	• Small things to fill—bucket, bowl, funnel • Things to undo—snaps, shoelaces, turning knobs, switches • Crayons, markers, watercolors, fingerpaints • Playdough	• Toy lawn mower or other push toys • Riding/peddling toys—scooter, trike • Wagon • Balls, bean bags

124

Playful Ways to Grow Strong

These playful suggestions help babies and toddlers develop large muscle skills. Pick activities that seem like a good match for your child's interest and abilities while keeping safety in mind. If the ideas seem too tough now, try again in a week or so. You may be surprised at how fast your baby develops. Toddlers and older preschoolers may find these activities exciting when they are done as part of an "obstacle course." Encourage your child with your enthusiasm and interest in their playful efforts to learn and grow. Applaud, laugh, participate or proudly sit back and watch as your little one gets stronger and smarter everyday!

Play That's Fun and Helps Baby Grow

- Roll baby on partially inflated beach ball. Place baby on his stomach on top of a beach ball. Carefully hold onto to him while you gently rock the ball back and forth. (This idea may also be helpful when trying to comfort a crying baby.)

- Encourage baby to hang onto parent's fingers and pull herself to a sitting or standing position.

- Put a plaything slightly out of reach and encourage baby to try to get the toy. Applaud and cheer for baby.

- Help baby crawl or walk between two pieces of furniture.

- Arrange pieces of furniture so baby can easily get from one to the other on her own.

- Put large pillows or you on the floor to climb or crawl over.

- Put a mattress on the floor to jump on and practice falling.

- Surround a low footstool with a pile of pillows to jump into. Or, collect a pile of leaves to jump into.

- Find or make toys that make sounds. Drums to pound, things to shake, xylophones to tap.

- Drape a small table with a blanket to hide under.

- Encourage trying out a toddler-sized slide. They have just a few steps to climb to reach a short slide.

- Have balls of several sizes to throw, kick or roll.

- Find or make a "walker" toy which baby can push ahead of her as she learns to walk. They give a beginning walker support and balance. (A small chair that can slide across the floor easily can make a good walker toy.)

(continued)

Playful Ways to Grow Strong *(continued)*

- Place pillows, cushions or folded blankets on a carpeted floor. Jump from one to another.

- Place large, sturdy cooking pots upside-down in a line. Use them as stepping stones.

- Make a tunnel to crawl through with big cardboard boxes or tables covered with blankets.

- Have "bean bags" to throw into a bucket or basket. (For easy bean bags, fill a clean sock part way with dry rice. Tie it very tight.)

- Older babies like to drop clothes pins into an open coffee can. To make it more challenging, cut a large hole in the plastic lid for the clothes pins to drop through.

- Set a large laundry basket on its side. Try to kick a ball into the basket.

- Encourage new ways of moving—walk or crawl backwards or sideways, turn in a circle, become all loose and wiggly and more.

- Lay a broom flat on the floor. Walk along the broom handle. Or, use a string or rope instead of the broom.

- Start to teach your toddler how to bounce a ball. (Most children won't be able to catch yet. A small, under-inflated beach ball can work well for beginners.)

- And best of all— mom or dad to playfully wrestle with, chase after, crawl over and hug.

© Meld 1999 • 612-332-7563

Child's Play: Toddlers Learn About Their World

Play is an important way children, especially toddlers, learn about the world. It may look like they're just having fun—and they are—but they are growing and developing, too. Play helps toddlers learn how the world works and how he fits into it. Play let's children try out and practice things they see—feeding a baby doll, making a car go, talking on the phone to grandpa. Toddlers love to explore, copy, pretend, repeat and more. It's often helps parents to understand how toddlers learn about their world through their play.

Know Your Baby

- Children will have a "play style" just as they have other styles. Some may prefer active, physical games, others would rather play quietly, still others prefer creative, dramatic play. Encourage your toddler to try all kinds of play.

- Crayons, paper, play dough, and other materials encourage creativity and develop small motor skills.

- Playing with dolls and stuffed animals helps kids develop emotionally as they copy your care for them and work out their feelings.

- Places to crawl, balls to throw, trikes to ride and other activities help baby's body grow.

- Imaginative play, like peek-a-boo or dress-up, lets kids practice language, social skills, and problem solving.

- Play builds self-esteem. Kids are free to do what they want and they are in control of the situation. They set the rules and limits. This is a great confidence builder because they cannot fail at what they do.

- Toddlers begin to be interested in the play of other kids. They aren't very skilled yet so don't expect them to be able to cooperate or share. This happens closer to age three. A toddler believes all things are his—if he's holding it, looked at it, touched it, or in any other way wanted it, it's his!

Know Yourself

- You can help your baby's development by joining in play, respecting his ideas for play, and encouraging his interests.

- Let loose with your playful side. This will make it easier for you to join in and will delight your child.

- How you participate in play will depend on your temperament and your child's. Not all parents and babies enjoy playing in the same way.

- Play can be messy. Decide what you can stand and find other ways for your child to play with mud or water or whatever you can't deal with.

- It's fine if you and baby's other parent play differently with your child. As a matter of fact, it benefits baby to learn a variety of styles.

Know the Situation

- The type of play that is OK may be determined by location—inside or outside, at home or away, for example.

- Living space affects play, but in most situations baby can have a small, private place to safely play and store toys and other playthings. Public parks and playgrounds for outdoor play space are just as much fun as private backyards.

- Create a safe, relaxed atmosphere for play. Childproof the play area and other areas so kids can explore freely. Constantly hearing "no" limits play and learning.

Look Who's Talking!

Baby's communicate from the time they are born. Their early communication, crying, may all sound alike to new parents. Soon, though, parents learn to tell a hungry cry from a sad cry. As baby grows, so will her language and ability to communicate. Here is a brief timetable for learning to talk. Remember, though, that there is a wide range of normal in child development. Some children are "wired" to talk earlier than others.

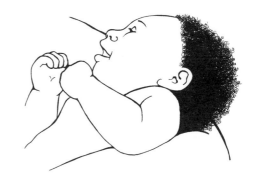

Learning to Talk?

Birth to 6 months
- Baby notices noises.
- Turns toward voice or sound, especially familiar voice of parent.
- Makes noise—oohing and cooing—other than crying.
- Laughs, chuckles.
- Squeals, bubbles.
- Around four months, starts to have give-and-take in "conversation."

6 to 12 Months
- Uses lips and tongue to make repetitive sounds—lalala or dadada.
- Puts vowel and consonant together.
- Repeats sounds made by parents.
- Changes in pitch and inflection makes babbling sound like talking.
- May say first recognizable word by nine months.

12 to 18 Months
- Says three words, other than "mama" or "dada".
- Points to body parts.
- Puts two words together.
- Uses one word to mean many things. "Dada" can mean daddy, boy, person, or that thing. All animals may be called cat.

18 to 24 Months
- Understands simple directions.
- Names pictures in book or magazine.
- Uses "no" to mean many things.
- Uses and misuses plurals.
- Starts to put things in categories—animals include dogs, cats, birds, cows.

About Ear Infections
Ear infections can interfere with learning to talk. A child who can't hear clearly will not be able to speak clearly. Any ear infection should be seen and treated by a doctor.

Are you concerned about your baby?
There is a wide range of normal for when children start to talk. Some children will begin early, while others may be two years old or older before uttering those first words. However, if you are exposing your child to language through talking and reading to her and she doesn't try to talk at all, or if she doesn't seem to understand anything you're saying to her, talk to your doctor. Early intervention is very important for language delays.

Baby Talk

Parents don't "teach" children to talk, but there are many ways parents can encourage language development. Here are a few suggestions that help with language development.

Does your family speak more than one language?

Expose baby to the sounds and rhythms of both. This is an important time because newborn and toddler brains are developing the ability to remember and repeat sounds and words. Your talking child may mix the words of both languages into the same sentence for awhile, but that's OK. Soon baby will know the difference.

Talk

The surest way to encourage language development, is to talk to your child. Before she can talk, she must understand language. She learns to understand it when she hears words used over and over in many ways. Tell baby how special she is, how much you love her, even if you think she doesn't understand your words. Baby will understand the "feeling" of your words and will connect with the warmth and love she hears in your voice. So, even if it seems silly to talk to someone who doesn't have a clue what you're saying, talk to your child.

Sing

Singing is another way to use language. Most children are naturally drawn to music. Sing along with a CD or tape of simple songs. Repetition increases language, so it's OK to sing the same songs over and over. Toddlers like repetition.

Read

Reading is a wonderful way to introduce children to language. Your child will love to hear the same stories over and over. Books with pictures of familiar things and those with catchy rhymes may be especially popular. It's never too early to start to read to your baby.

Listen

When baby "talks" to you, listen with care. Even if you can't understand what he's saying, you encourage him by paying attention and responding to his conversation.

Label

Toddlers have to learn all the words in their language one at a time! You can help her by labeling out loud the many things in her world. Name what you see on the playground, at home, in books, wherever you are. This helps her understand that words have meaning.

Question

Even before a toddler can answer, asking questions is a good way to encourage language development. Asking what book he wants to read or which snack to eat gives your baby chance to use his words. Don't overdo it, though. Too many questions can stress him out.

Repeat, Repeat, Repeat

Repeating what your toddler says in different words—A ball? You want the red ball?—Shows you understand what she is saying and gives you the chance to expand her language and pronunciation.

(continued)

© Meld 1999 • 612-332-7563

Baby Talk *(continued)*

Word Power: Tips for Talkers

- Repeat baby's coos and babbles. Pause after you say something so baby has time to respond.

- Look baby in the eye when you talk or sing to her.

- Make up songs and rhymes using baby's name.

- Talk about what you see, hear and smell. Say, "I smell cookies," or "Doesn't the lotion smell good?"

- Make your conversation more complex as baby grows. Babies understand more than they can say.

- Avoid the temptation to just talk in "baby talk." It's cute to call that blanket the "baba," but it doesn't help build your baby's vocabulary.

- Expand your child's one word phrases. When he says "ball," you say, "Yes, it's a red ball" or "Ball rolls."

- If you can't understand what your child is saying, guess.

- Help your child find the words he is looking for. Fill in the "blanks" if he seems to need some help.

- Explain what different words mean. When you are on a walk, point to flowers as you say, "Flower," touch a tree when you say, "Tree" and pat the grass when you say "Grass."

- Look at and read books to your baby as often as you can. Find a few simple picture books you both like and snuggle up for some very special and important time together.

- When looking at books, offer chances for your older baby to "read" by saying something like, "Here is a soft kitty. What do kitties say?"

- Your child will be very interested in watching and listening to you talk with others. Give her chances to learn by overhearing your conversations. But remember, she will probably want to join in and may interrupt you—that's just what toddlers do!

- Play listening games. Sit close to each other and say, "Shhh, listen carefully. Can you hear…" (the bird, fire truck, baby cry).

- Waiting—in doctor's office, for the bus, wherever—is a good time for playing word games. Take turns rhyming words (don't worry too much whether the rhyme is a "real" word).

- Puppets can have conversations about many things—with each other and with kids and adults.

130

© Meld 1999 • 612-332-7563

What a Toddler Understands

When your child begins to talk, it doesn't mean he can understand everything he hears. You can help the communication between you by keeping these things in mind.

Toddlers need the whole picture

Use props. Point. If you want him to put his shoes away, pick up the shoes, point to the child's bedroom and say, "Let's put your shoes in your bedroom." Watch and help him complete the activity.

Toddlers vary day-to-day in what they understand

One day she might understand what "broccoli" means and the next day act like she's never heard the word.

Toddlers can't make logical connections

A child might not understand, "If you don't put on your boots, you can't go outside." It's too complicated. "We wear boots outside," is easier for him to understand.

Toddlers may sometimes "read between the lines"

Toddlers often understand what we intend, even when we don't say it. They hear "Go back to bed" when we say "Are you up again?"

Children hear literally

A child's mind pictures exactly what you are saying. "Daddy's tied up at school." "I wonder where the scissors walked off to?" "You have a frog in your throat." Expect some confusion when you use such phrases, but don't avoid them. They are a colorful, fun part of our language. You can explain what each phrase means, and enrich your child's language.

Children learn at their own pace

All children eventually learn to talk, but each will learn at his own pace. Boys may talk later than girls. Children who are around adults may speak earlier than those raised with other children. Early talkers are not smarter or more clever than later talkers, any more than early walkers will win every race they run.

The number of words children know varies

Most children speak one to ten words by 12 months, 100 words at two and up to 300 words by three. Children often understand far more words than they can say. If by age three your child's speech seems to lag behind others his age or he doesn't seem to hear or understand things you say, talk to your doctor. Ask to have your child's hearing checked. He may have some hearing loss.

(continued)

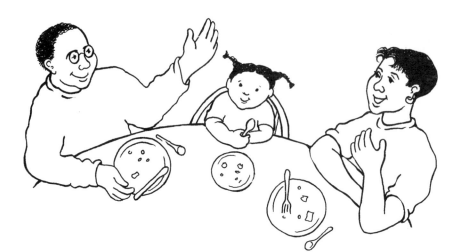

Bilingual Families

Children from families who regularly speak two languages may at first say fewer words, but will soon catch up. Bilingual children may also combine words of both languages. Don't worry, she will soon be able to sort them out and put the words to the same language together. Teaching baby both languages will eventually be an asset for your child. At this young age, children learn and remember the sounds and rhythms of words the very best.

One word often says it all and may express a complete thought

"Bobby" might mean, "Here comes my cousin, he's going to lift me out of the highchair, we'll tumble on the floor and have fun."

Memory is expanding

Your child might start talking about things that aren't in the room or things that happened last week. His memory is expanding. But this doesn't mean he remembers everything that happened a few days ago.

Toddlers often think out loud

Eventually, self-direction becomes silent and your child will only use "out loud" talk to communicate with others.

When a child begins to put two words together, she is beginning to create her own language

She will probably go from naming a thing (doggie) to noticing where a thing is (doggie there), where it isn't (doggie gone) or what belongs to whom (my doggie) to what things and people can do (doggie sits). This language progression is the same across many cultures and many languages.

"Are You Listening?" How to Talk to Your Child

Communication is a two-way street. We can talk all we want, but if no one is listening, there is no communication. Parents can be frustrated when their child seems to ignore what they're saying.

Using simple courtesy and these approaches make it more likely that your child will listen.

- Be sure you have her attention. If she is busy playing, kindly interrupt her before you begin saying what you want her to hear.

- Use the same rules you expect your child to use, such as not yelling or shouting. If you would like him to do something, go where your child is and ask him to do it.

- Be polite to your child. Say "please," and "thank you," or "excuse me." Be a good role model for baby.

- Don't interrupt your child when she's talking. Listen to her.

- Speak at eye level. Direct eye contact helps get your point across. You can tell if he is listening and understands what you say. You can stoop down and talk to your child or pick him up.

- Use simple words, phrases and body language that she understands.

- Talk about one subject at a time.

- Repeat what you're saying as often as necessary. Try saying the same thing in different ways, so he can understand what you are trying to tell him.

- She will be more apt to listen to you when you speak with affection and understanding.

- When you explain something to your child, don't assume what you say will transfer to other situations. If you say, "Don't write on the walls," your child will apply what you've said to the walls in question, not to the walls in another room or to the floor. By saying, "We only write on paper," you give your child a limit he can apply easily in other situations.

- Avoid having too many rules. Your child won't be able to understand or remember them all.

- Give her clear, first-things-first directions. "Take your shoes off, and put them into the closet."

- Take care not to give one message with your words and another with your body posture, tone of voice, or facial expression.

- Don't unkindly criticize your child—be supportive and respectful. Take her efforts seriously and don't make fun of or tease about her efforts and activities.

- Be a good listener. Pay attention to your child when he talks to you.

133

Growing Up: Steps Towards Independence

As babies grow into toddlers, parents will see their child taking steps toward being their own person. We all want our children to grow up knowing the skills needed to take good care of themselves. This process begins when babies are young and continues for years as more skills are learned. Parents can encourage independence when they understand their child and understand their own responses to their child's new independence.

Know Your Baby

- No one is born able to do everything for himself. We must be taught what is expected of us. Developing these skills takes time. Some children may easily learn these skills. Other may require more deliberate teaching.

- A baby with a temperament that makes him easily distracted may need more help and coaching to learn to help himself. A persistent baby may have an easier time learning.

- Learn about what your child can be expected to do. This will vary from child to child and will change with age, but here are some possibilities:
  - Telling you what she needs.
  - Cooperating when getting him dressed.
  - Feeding herself.
  - Not hitting.
  - Using words to express feelings.
  - Start getting himself dressed even if clothes don't match.

- Most children will need reinforcement, praise, and encouragement as they are learning independence skills.

- As children get older, we want them to learn to praise and appreciate themselves for doing the right thing and not rely as much on praise and encouragement from others.

Know Yourself

- Visualize the future—your child as a responsible adult who can hold a job, take care of herself (and others, if needed), make wise choices, and more, begins as a child is being taught and coached by her parents. Patience, repetition and more are required in order to help kids develop into people who can do it themselves.

- Your temperament will guide your child towards independence. If you are easily distracted from a chore and never finish it, your child will come to think that's the way things are done.

- Don't stand in the way of growing independence by never offering a child a choice or a chance to make a decision.

Know the Situation

- Because a child's ability to remember to do something depends on routines and familiarity, any change in routine can affect how well she remembers or does a task.

"Me Do It!" Toddler Independence

Toddlers are starting to be more independent, pulling away from parents and becoming their own persons. A big part of this is their desire to do more for themselves. They want to feed themselves, dress themselves, and make choices. After all , everyone likes to be able to slip off pajamas, pour some more milk or pick out their own special story book to read. There may be some drawbacks to independence. For example, a child may worry parents won't love him if he is so independent and parents may feel a sense of loss of the total caregiver role or impatience at the slowness of a toddler buttoning up. This independence is a positive step toward growing up that parents can encourage.

Readiness to do things alone depends on your child's:

- Large and small muscle development.

- Understanding of cause and effect.

- Temperament — Is your child patient or easily frustrated? (See pages 113-115.)

- Desire to be independent.

An 18 to 24-month-old child wants to be independent

Doing it herself is important to a child as she gets older. As she grows up, she wants to:

- Turn on the TV, radio or stereo.

- Wash her own hands.

- Help you cook. Or cook herself.

- Walk outside without holding onto your hand.

- Brush her teeth (and maybe yours).

- Sweep, mop, dust, vacuum, hammer, shovel, scoop or rake.

- Blow her own nose.

- Choose her own playthings or story book.

- Kiss her own hurts.

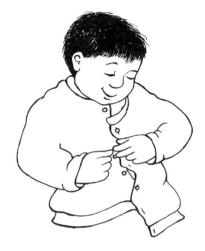

- Put on and take off her clothes.

- Drink from a cup and use a spoon.

- Decide for himself when to get out of the bathtub.

Let your child do as many things as she is safely able to do. Make her feel important and responsible for what she can accomplish. But say no to things that could hurt her.

Promoting Independence

Parents play the key role in promoting or discouraging independence. Show child how to do a task and then stand back and let him try it. Don't jump in and take over unless his struggles seem to be turning to anger or frustration.

Be Patient

- It usually takes more time for your child to do something than it does to do it yourself. Practice patience when teaching a child to do something, whether how to put on his coat or how to stack blocks. Your child will repeat routines hundreds of times before she masters a task.

- Try to work with your child when you have time, not when you're rushed or feeling pressured.

- Be patient when your child's explorations lead to more work for you—spilled milk or shoes on the wrong feet are a small price for an independent child who feels proud of what she can do.

(continued)

© Meld 1999 • 612-332-7563

"Me Do It!" Toddler Independence *(continued)*

Observe
- By watching your child, you'll know when he is able to use a fork or clean up a spill. You'll also be able to tell when he is in over his head.
- Children don't always know when to ask for help. Be there for him, but don't interfere until you see he really needs help or he asks for it.

Make It Easy
- Buy shoes and clothes that slip on and off easily—Velcro® is a big help.
- Put hooks, shelves and drawers within your child's reach so she can put things away.
- A sturdy stool by the bathroom sink helps washing and brushing go more easily.
- Serve finger foods or foods that are easy to eat with a spoon.

Develop Routines
- Have routines so your child can develop good habits. Make it part of the day that toys go back in the toy box when playing is done, dirty clothes go in the hamper, dishes are carried to the sink.
- By starting now, when your toddler wants to help, makes pitching in and helping out a habit later on.

Use Simple Directions
- Give your child clear, simple, step-by-step directions. Use as few words as possible.
- Show her how to do the task in two or three simple steps, then let her try it herself. Remember, there is more than one way to do something.
- Parents should focus on the outcome—did the task get done—more than the steps to get there.
- And remember, efficiency is much more important to parents than it is to toddlers.
- Applaud efforts. Be generous with praise.

Safe and Restful Sleep

Babies need their sleep, just as adults do, to maintain their energy and to have adequate rest do they can grown and develop. Some babies may be considered "good" sleepers—go to bed easily, stay asleep—while others may need help because they wake often, fuss at bedtime, or mix up night and day. Whichever your baby is, the following are ways to make sure baby gets the rest he needs.

Also see page 50 for more about sleep and bedtime routines.

The safest sleeping position for young babies is on their backs. This positions helps prevent Sudden Infant Death Syndrome (SIDS).

Cozy sleeping space

- A crib is a great place for baby to sleep, but some newborns, find a crib too big for comfort. Newborns can sleep in other safe places—a carefully-padded cardboard box, drawer, laundry basket, bassinet—as long as it's warm and safe.
- Some breastfeeding moms take baby into bed with them. The advantage is not having to get up in the middle of the night to feed the baby. In addition to adult beds being dangerous for baby because of the possibility of falls and suffocation, the disadvantages can include loss of sleep and privacy.
- Older babies who are starting to crawl need to be protected from falling out of the crib. Lower the crib mattress whenever baby can get her arms over the top.
- Keep a sleeping baby away from pets, drafts, loud noises and other young children.

Movement

- Babies enjoy rhythmic movement. Rocking, swinging, or swaying can bring on sleep.

Comfortable temperature

- Being too warm or cold can make it hard for baby to sleep. Be sure baby is dressed both for the room temperature and for the amount of blankets.
- Pajamas with feet can eliminate the need for covers in some weather, although some babies need the weight of the covers to feel secure enough to sleep.

Sound

- For the first nine months, baby was soothed by mom's heartbeat and other interior sounds. It may be difficult for your baby to sleep without some noise now.
- Try the "white" noise of a fan. Soft music from a music box or radio can help.

A place of her own

- Baby sleeps best in an area that's not shared with her parents, not so much because your presence will disturb her but because you're likely to pick her up at the first sound. This interrupts her regular sleeping pattern. Parents need to be close enough to hear her cries before she gets frantic, but she needs to be able to settle on her own too.

Routine

- A bedtime routine is soothing to baby. Even though an infant may fall asleep while nursing or feeding, by six months you can begin a bedtime ritual which will signal sleep is just around the corner.
- Routines can include a warm bath, putting on pajamas, singing or reading, and being tucked in. (See page 50.)

Daytime rest

- Babies, even those who have nighttime sleeping problems, need naps to ensure they get all the rest they need.
- Babies who don't nap may be so overtired in the evening they can't settle down to sleep.

Bedtime Blues: What's the Problem?

Bedtime blues can come at any age and for many reasons. If you know your child, know yourself and know the situation, you can figure out ways to deal with the blues you're facing.

Know Your Baby

- Bedtime means separation for children—from parents, from their activities, from the life of the home—and entrance into a world of isolation, stillness and darkness. It can be scary and unsettling.

- Some children may be born to be "good sleepers" while others seem to have problems falling asleep from infancy on. Acceptance of this part of the child is an important step toward solving or accepting the situation.

- Each child's need for sleep varies. Infants sleep more than toddlers (12 to 13 hours a day) or preschoolers (10 to 12 hours a day).

- Some children may be night owls—active at night and slow in the morning. Parents can tell how much sleep a baby needs—does baby seem well-rested or irritable? How does he act if he has more or less sleep?

- Daytime sleeping—naps—can interfere with bedtime as baby gets older.

- Developmental changes may affect sleep. As children grow, their approach to all parts of life, including sleeping, may change. Toddlers and preschoolers are starting to assert independence from parents—they want to control their own lives, which can include when, where and how much they sleep.

- Learning how to comfort oneself, calm down and go to sleep are important independence skills all must learn. A child can learn to rely on herself, not something "outside"—being rocked to sleep, needing to be fed a bottle, etc.—to get to sleep.

Know Yourself

- Parents are often tired at the end of the day and don't want hassles and conflicts. Parents want some private time, time for themselves and may have guilty feelings about wanting their child to go to bed. Parents may also feel the need to spend more time with baby. How a parent feels can affect how he deals with a child's sleep.

- Parents can keep in mind that it's their responsibility to put baby to bed (and to provide a safe, secure place for her to sleep) but it's the child's job to actually do the sleeping. Parents can't **make** baby sleep, they can only do the things that will help baby sleep.

- Understand your own sleep needs. Are you a lark (up early, chipper, ready to go) or an owl (go to bed late, sleep in)? How do you fit with your child? Is this a source of the conflict?

Know the Situation

- Is there a change in family life that might cause bedroom blues? Maybe a change in babysitters, a move, an illness, different schedule, visitors, etc.?

- Was there a trigger—something which seemed to start the sleeping problem or bedtime issues?

- Is the sleeping space comfortable and secure? Quiet, dimly lit, the same routine every night?

Sleep Problems? How to Help Baby

Even with parents' careful thought and preparation, baby can experience sleep problems. Here are some ideas for ways to handle common sleep problems.

Newborns

A newborns may seem to have day and night reversed.

What to do:
- Keep daytime sleeping to no more than three to four hours at a time. Try to keep baby up a little longer during the day.
- After the last evening feeding, begin a simple bedtime routine to let baby know it's bedtime. (See page 50 for more about routines.)

6 to 18 Months Old

Changes in baby's growth and development at this age may cause changes at bedtime—she is much more aware and sensitive. Being too tired by new activities, changes in routines, overstimulated by increasing awareness of her environment and more may make it difficult for baby to settle down.

What to do:
- Learn the signals that she is tired—rubbing her eyes or her ear, sucking her thumb. Plan ahead to catch her before she becomes overtired and has trouble settling down.

- Stick to your established bedtime routine.

Teething pain may now make sleeping difficult.

What to do:
- Before bedtime try gently rubbing baby's gums with a small ice cube wrapped in a clean, damp cloth. Or, let baby chew on a cold "teething ring."
- Ask your doctor if an infant non-aspirin pain reliever would help. There are also ointments that can be rubbed on baby's gums that temporarily numb the pain. Before trying, ask your doctor if these are good for your baby.

At this age, baby is old enough to resist a sleeping routine. She is beginning to go through separation anxiety, too—the fear of being away from parents. Other things can trigger sleep problems, such as a break in routine during a vacation, a move into a new living space, teething or an illness.

What to do:
- Increase her physical activity during the day. Go swimming or take a walk around the block in the evening.
- Make sure she is tired. Does she need a daytime nap or do you need that naptime? Can she give up a daytime nap so she's tired at night?
- Make the hour before nap or bedtime pleasant and calming. A child won't be ready to settle down after a rousing game of hide-and-go-seek. Eliminate as much stimulation as possible.
- Lengthen the nightly routine so he has more time to bridge the gap between day and night. After a bath, give him some time to play quietly or read a book. He will understand bedtime is coming, but he has more of a chance to get used to the idea.
- If your child cries, respond by going in

(continued)

Sleep Problems? How to Help Baby *(continued)*

the room and saying "good night." Let her know the day is over, and getting out of bed isn't an option. Be businesslike about it—don't offer food or other rewards to bribe the child to go to sleep.

• Put a stuffed animal, book or soft toy in the crib or bed. If there's enough light from a night light or hallway light, the child can play himself to sleep.

Toddlers

Toddlers are becoming more independent and want to control their world and what happens to them. One thing they want to control is when they sleep.

What to do:
• Make sure your child is tired. It's hard to settle down before you're ready.

• Use whatever soothing bedtime routines you have always used.

• Give some choices so he has some control. Let him choose which book to read, which

pajamas, whether the night light will be on, which toys will join him in bed and other simple choices.

• Be firm that it's not a choice not to go to bed.

• Explain that it's OK if she plays in bed before sleeping, but it must be quiet play and no getting up.

If Baby Wakes In the Middle of the Night

• Give baby a few minutes to comfort himself if you hear only a few sounds.

• Check the basics—wet diaper, too warm or cold, not feeling well, thirsty, afraid and more.

• Comfort baby in her own bed. Try a minute of gently rubbing her arm, tummy or head, tucking in, saying good night and then leaving the room.

Rise & Shine!

Going to bed's not the problem with some toddlers, it's getting up at the crack of dawn! What can you do?

• Decide how you feel about this—is it OK if he's up and about because that means you must be, too!

• If you are busy or groggy in the early morning, be sure that your entire home, is completely child-proofed. You may want to use a gate to keep her in or out of certain rooms.

• Make it safe for baby to get out of bed. Put a chair next to the crib and teach him how to climb out safely. Or put his mattress on the floor.

If you don't want her up, try these things:
• Respond when she cries. If she knows you're always available, she won't have the need to come to you.

• Be sure no climbing furniture—chairs, tables, desks—are near the crib to assist him in getting out.

• Lower crib mattress so it's more difficult for baby to get out.

Toilet Training

The mark of childhood independence most sought by parents is using the toilet. Mountains of advice from grandparents, friends, neighbors and others is available for the asking. But be patient, there is no rush. Most experts recommend waiting until baby is over two years of age. If there is a last word on the subject, it's that a child will be able to use the toilet only when he is good and ready.

Signs of Readiness

Most child development experts say to wait until a child is over two years old to start toilet training. Before that age, baby is just not ready. Be sure you see two or more of these signs before beginning any toilet training.

Shows some bladder control

- Urinates a lot at one time, rather than dribbling.
- Stays dry for several hours.
- Tells you with a facial expression or posture that he is about to go to the bathroom.
- Seems to notice when he is urinating.

Is ready physically

- Can easily pick up objects with fingers.
- Can walk from room to room easily, without help.
- Can sit down and get up.
- Can make her wants known with words or clear actions

Can follow directions and copy

- Points to nose, eyes, mouth or hair when asked.
- If asked, can sit down or walk to another place.
- Imitates you with pat-a-cake, peek-a-boo and more.
- Can bring you a familiar toy.
- Wants to be clean and likes to have clean hands and clothes.
- Wants to please you.
- Wants to be independent.
- Notices when you go to the bathroom, wash your face and brush your teeth— and wants to imitate you.

Toilet Training Hints

- Don't train your child when the two of you are having trouble, such as when your toddler is negative much of the time or you feel impatient.
- Wait until your child is ready. If you try to train your child too soon, it's you who are trained.
- Toilet training is not a race. Don't let your mother, neighbor or anyone else tell you when you "ought" to train your child.
- Most children are not ready for training until they are two years old or older. Boys are often slower than girls.
- If you start training your child and it gets to be a hassle, stop for awhile and come back to it in a week or two.

(continued)

Toilet Training *(continued)*

Wetting the Bed

Few children under the age of three years old are capable of controlling their bladders during the night. Night time diapers may still be necessary. If your child starts waking up in the morning with a dry diaper and urinates only once in four hours during the day, try replacing a diaper with a pair of thick cotton training pants.

Your child may still prefer to wear a diaper at night. That's OK—it's easier to change a diaper than to wash sheets. When you think your child is capable of having a dry night, try the following ideas:

- Don't restrict evening beverages—a thirsty child may have other sleeping problems. But, don't offer too many either.

- If she wets the bed, don't make her feel ashamed. Let her help you take the sheets off the bed, and involve her in the clean up.

- If your child starts wetting the bed after a long period of dryness, determine if bed-wetting is due to anxiety or stress.

- Remain calm—don't overreact. If necessary, call a friend who's been through the experience, and discuss your frustrations with her.

- Bed-wetting shouldn't be considered a problem until after the child is seven years old. Talk to your doctor if you are concerned.

Helping Children Behave

The first step to helping children behave is to understand your child and yourself. If you can get a clear picture of what your child is capable of doing—or not doing—it's easier to understand why she is reacting the way she is. Look at yourself, too, and why you might react as you do when your child misbehaves. Looking at each situation makes it possible to plan ahead for possible problems and make changes to head them off.

Know Your Baby

- Babies and toddlers cannot control their actions, even if just told not to do something. They don't do this to make parents mad, they're just developmentally unable to control their actions and behavior.

- Three year olds are just beginning to be able to control their behavior. If told not to touch, they may start, but stop themselves. Or, they may do something, such as dropping their food on the floor all the while saying, "No, no, no." They sort of remember your expectation about throwing food, but it's still hard to put your rule with the actions and then use self-control to stop their behavior.

- Learning to talk helps children behave and to develop self-control. This gives them the words to remind themselves of what to do. It also helps them express their feelings — "I want to go home!"

- Few children go directly from happy and sunny to a complete breakdown. Learn the signals that your child is reaching his max and pay attention when you see them.

- Have realistic expectations. Know what you can expect your child to be able to do at different ages. Learn as much as you can about child development and temperament. Ask other parents about their experiences and how they handle problems with behavior.

Know Yourself

- Listen to your child when she lets you know about her needs. You can urge your toddler to "use words" to express her feelings but even before words develop, pay attention to your child's other signals and respond.

- Children eventually learn that different places have different rules. Parents help by talking about what is expected in different situations and by gently, but consistently, guiding baby's actions.

- Perhaps, most important of all, keep in mind that baby loves you and wants to be just like you. Be a good role model— show your child how to behave and get along well in the world.

Know the Situation

- Tiredness, hunger, health, time of day, etc. affect both parents and children and may cause you to change plans or cut an outing short.

- Look at what it is about the situation that might trigger unwanted behavior. Look at things from baby's point of view. Too many people, too much confusion or too high of expectations can lead to unwanted behavior.

- Young children have not yet developed the ability to ignore or shut out all the things going on around them. When there are lots of bright lights, noises, smells or temperature changes, it can get to be too much for little ones. Everything may seem fine to you but baby can experience "sensory overload" which may lead to unwanted behavior.

Setting the Stage for Good Behavior

No one, not even the most inexperienced parent, thinks children naturally know how to behave. One of the most important jobs parents have is teaching children what behavior will help them get along well at home and out in the world. In addition to making life easier on all, guiding a child's behavior shows the child that he is important and that his parents care about him.

Before parents can begin to teach and guide baby towards behavior they prefer, it helps to have an understanding of what a child is capable of at different ages.

Birth to 18 months

In the first few weeks, baby is learning about her new world. She is far from ready for even the simplest lessons in behavior. It's these early days, however, that the foundation of good behavior is set. The foundation starts with the love, kisses, gentle care, and more that parents give to baby over and over again. As baby consistently receives this loving care, she learns to trust, to know that you are there for her, and to turn to your for love, encouragement and approval.

As baby develop, she begins to exchange smiles and "talks" with you. By two months, she will be responding to the expressions of your face and voice. She will start to imitate you. This is important because it's a key way young children learn about the behavior others expect.

By nine months, babies are just beginning to understand the word no. But this doesn't mean they will stop what they are doing when you say "no-no". They don't yet have much self-control. At this point, distraction is the best thing to try.

After nine months, baby may respond to simple requests. Words such as "give me the ball," or "sit still" gives baby her first chances to mind you— an important step toward learning how to behave.

Walking brings more independence and demands for freedom. This stage introduces frustration, too, as she realizes she can't have everything she wants, when she wants it. She may express her feelings by hitting or throwing things. Keep in mind this is very typical. Stay calm, firmly tell baby that "we don't hit others" and then move her and redirect her attention to something else less frustrating.

18 months to 3 years

Toddlers have learned the difference between "yours" and "mine." You will hear "mine" often as your child starts to discover more about what his world has to offer.

A second development is the independence shown by use of the word "NO!" "No" can be the most common work in baby's vocabulary, used to show his demand for independence and control. You may hear "no shoes!", "no bed!", "no eat!" Frustration at having his "nos" objected to can lead to tantrums.

All this resistance and testing is part of the natural pulling away from parents and becoming his own person. Try to find ways to set limits on his behavior and encourage cooperation while respecting his need for independence.

Toddlers learn about good behavior best when given clear rules and a save place for him to learn to behave within those rules. Tempting objects should not be put in his way. Prevention and distraction is often the most best way to teach at this age. (See pages 145-147.)

Toddlers do have flashes of cooperation and concern for others' feelings. Parents should recognize these efforts and praise them as helpful signs of social growth.

Preventing Misbehavior

"An ounce of prevention is worth a pound of cure" is an old saying that works for misbehavior, too. By creating an atmosphere and environment that encourages good behavior and eliminates a lot of opportunity for misbehavior, parents can make life easier and more pleasant for the entire family.

Tell your child what your expect
With positive words, let your child know what the limit is. Avoid always saying, "No-No" or "Don't." For example, "We sit in our chairs when we eat meals." Or, "We pet Kitty with open hands."

Have realistic expectations
Until age three, children are unable to control most of their behavior. Remember your child is still a child. (See pages 143-144 for more information.)

Remove objects and situations which may be too tempting for your child
Put away things which you don't want touched, cover furniture which shouldn't be climbed on, lock cupboard doors which shouldn't be opened. Some parents find it's a good idea to leave one safely child-proofed cupboard for baby to play with and in when he chooses.

Have opportunities for active physical play
Make a safe place for baby to be able to be active, inside as well as outside. Know about child development, child-proof the area and find ways to adapt things in baby's world so that he can successfully roll, crawl, run, jump and more. So, just in case your child wants to jump on the bed, which may be off limits, there is an acceptable alternative such as cushions on the floor.

Catch your child being good
Let your child know what things she is doing that please you. This encourages good behavior.

Use kindness and touch
A misbehaving or out of control child may be settled down by a gentle touch or calm voice. Kindly, but firmly, encourage him to behave. Sometimes a hug is all that is needed for a misbehaving child to regain control.

Distract
For example, a child about to use a toy or other object in a destructive way may be stopped by having you ask to see the toy. Then suggest and show her ways she can use it that aren't destructive.

Laugh together
Try humor with a toddler or preschooler who is about to burst with anger and frustration. This offers the child an opportunity to "save face." Remember to be kind with your humor and not tease your child into tears.

Tell your child how you are feeling and ask for cooperation
For example, "That noise is too loud for inside. Let's find something else you can do or we can go outside." Even very young children who cannot understand exactly what a parent is saying can make some sense out of comments like this.

Explain situations
Help the child understand the cause of his frustration or why the rule is there. But use just a few very simple words and phrases.

Role model good behavior
Be the kind of person you want your child to become. You have enormous influence over what kind of person your child will be. He wants to be just like you!

What Is Discipline?

Discipline can be best thought of as a way to guide, protect and teach your child. It's important because the end result is a child who:

- **knows ways to cooperate and get along in the world.**
- **is safe and protected.**
- **has high self-esteem and self-control.**
- **understands how to adjust and adapt successfully.**
- **is confident because his world is predictable and people care about him.**

Sometimes discipline is thought to mean punishment. Many parents have learned that yelling, spanking and shaming children doesn't help them grow into successful adults. Keep in mind that guidance and discipline require parents' patience, love, time, willingness to learn about child development and commitment to teach their child helpful ways to behave.

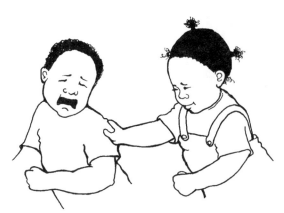

Some Things to Keep in Mind

Set limits
Children like limits on their behavior. It makes him feel safe and secure because he knows what you expect of him. Limits for young children are meant to keep them safe. As little ones grow, the rules will change. Limits should be reasonable, appropriate to the age of the child, and stated in a way he can understand them. So you can say, "We don't hit people with our toys." If the behavior doesn't stop, you can say, "We'll put the toy away so you can't use it to hit others."

Setting basic limits and enforcing them can begin when child is around nine months old. At that age, limits should be designed to keep her safe.

Discipline positively
Use simple words and a kind, but firm, voice. Parents don't need to yell or hit to get the point across. When possible, use "please do this," instead of "don't do that."

Praise and encourage
These are effective ways to help children behave.

Kids want to please parents and respond best to your love, praise and encouragement.

Discipline consistently
It's not fair to follow through on a rule one day and let it slide the next. This will confuse your child and make him doubt that you really mean what you say.

Give reasons for rules
Explain in a way your young child can understand about why the rule is there. "Because I'm the parent," may not be the best reason to give to your child to help him understand the actions. Say, "We don't hit others because it hurts them."

Discipline is not something that is usually appropriate to start until around nine months of age. Until then, baby is just too young to understand and remember. Even at that age, guidance and discipline needs to be very simple, kind and gentle.

Don't belittle or humiliate your child
Discipline in private when possible. Discipline shouldn't shame or embarrass your child. It should guide and correct.

Don't wait
Discipline and correct as soon as the misbehavior happens. This is most effective in changing behavior. Young children's memories are short. It will confuse him if he is suddenly, in his mind, disciplined for something he can't even remember.

Check on your methods
Be sure to watch your child to see how she reacts to the discipline method. You want to be sure the method you use to guide and correct is understood and is having the affect you want. (See page 147 for methods to try.)

146

Discipline Methods That Work

There are many positive methods of discipline that work as baby becomes a toddler and preschooler. Parents can choose those that are best for their child and family. The methods and ideas listed here work with children of different ages, but parents should adapt the methods to the age, the misbehavior and the temperament of the child.

About Young Babies

Keep in mind that until a child is nine months or older, the best "discipline" method is to remove a child from a situation or to change the situation. At nine months, a child is only beginning to understand limits and "no."

A Note About Spanking

Spanking is generally considered an inappropriate method. It gives the wrong message—that might is right—and doesn't provide a long-term solution to changing behavior.

Notice and praise good behavior

Catch your child doing something you like and let him know. This reinforces good behavior and shows him that good behavior gets attention, too. This method works with kids of all ages.

Distraction

Try directing baby's attention away from the problem. Point out another interesting toy or something else to turn your child's attention away from what he's doing or wanting. Try trading one thing for another, "This magazine is mommy's. Here's one for Chaka."

Ignore the behavior

Not every incident requires discipline. If there is no danger to your child or someone else, it may be better to let it go. Constant correction can interfere with your child's ability to decide how to behave on her own.

Structure the environment

A physically safe environment—childproofed, with temptations out of sight—eliminates a lot of misbehavior. The predictable structure of simple rules helps him learn how to behave.

Control the situation, not the child

Look at the situation from the child's point of view and make changes to avoid any problems. Baby may not understand that it's not OK to dig through and dump out your backpack. Keep things that baby can't play with out of reach to avoid problems.

Offer choices

Even the youngest toddler likes to express his independence by making choices. She may feel more cooperative when asked to choose between things, instead of having one chosen for her. Not everything can be a choice, however. Issues of safety, such as sitting in the car seat, are never a choice.

Plan ahead

This can avoid a lot of behavior problems. Think ahead about the situation and make choices and/or changes that lead to good behavior—or at least don't invite bad. Shopping when baby is well-rested will be more pleasant for everyone than by going at naptime.

Let child experience consequences

Experiencing the consequences helps toddlers start to understand how their behavior affects their lives. Consequences should be safe though. It's not OK for kids to experience the consequences of going into the street and getting hit by a car. It is OK for a child to have a special toy put away for awhile for mistreating it.

Stay consistent

Following through on a rule one day, but letting it slide the next will confuse a child. She will not know when the rule will be enforced and when it won't. After awhile, she will ignore all the rules and take her chances on whether you will respond or not. It's not possible to be 100 percent consistent, but parents can try.

Exclude child with time out

"Time out" is the brief removal of a misbehaving child from being with others. It works best for those old enough to understand about rules and consequences (about age three). Limit the time out to a few minutes—usually one minute per year of the age of the child.

Problem Solving: Step-by-Step

Parents often have the information and skills they need to solve a problem, but sometimes it helps to have a step-by-step plan when laying out all the information. Problem solving is a skill that can be used many times throughout your life. It can help with problems you might have with your child, your child care provider, baby's other parent, family members and more.

Young children can start to be involved in simple problem solving once they can talk and understand what's being said—around three years old. Parents will need to help him express his thoughts and feelings and suggest possible solutions at first. After some practice, he can make suggestions, and even offer some parents haven't thought of. Parent and child can decide together what to do, then see if it works, and choose another solution if it doesn't. The steps in problem solving with children are the same as in all problem solving, but parents need to teach these rather than assume children just know how to do it.

1. Identify and name the problem

Gather information about your child, yourself, the situation and anything you may need to know—who is involved, how long has it been going on, etc. State the problem clearly. For example, "My child won't nap anymore."

2. Talk about how it affects each person involved

Let everyone express his feelings about the problem, including why it is or is not a problem in his view. Why is giving up naps a problem? How does it affect your child? Others?

3. Think of possible solutions

Brainstorm about different ideas. Be imaginative and creative. What can you do about the "no nap" problem. Would a quiet time work, later bedtime or more exercise make a difference?

4. Reach an agreement or compromise

Select one of the solutions that is agreeable to everyone and that you all agree might work. Decide what you will try and for how long.

5. Try it out. Did the solution help?

Not everything will work the first or even the fifth time. Decide how long you will try this before you decide if it will work or not. Then look at the results and decide what, if anything, needs to be changed. In the nap case, you may need to try several approaches.

6. Keep trying

Do each step as many times as you need to so you can find a solution that works. Or, in the nap example, you might decide it's not a problem.

"She's Gonna Snap!" Coping With Temper Tantrums

It's a rare toddler who doesn't have at least one tantrum. Temper tantrums can occur at any time, any place. Before you snap (not the thing to do), try to understand why your toddler is upset and what can be done to prevent tantrums. And, then, if prevention doesn't work, learn what to do during the temper tantrum.

Your toddler might react the way you react when you're angry. If you scream and throw things, chances are your child will do the same. Show baby appropriate ways of expressing anger so she can learn from your good example.

The Cause

Tantrums often result from frustration. A toddler may head toward a tantrum if:

- She can't decide what to do because she's been given too many choices.
- He can't get his body to do the things he wants it to do.
- She is dependent on you but wants to be independent.
- He is being asked to do too much, too soon, too fast. Or visa versa.
- She is tired, hungry, off schedule.
- He is having difficulty understanding something (why the top block keeps falling off the tower).

Preventing

Try to prevent temper tantrums before they occur. Here are a few ideas:

- Don't put your child in situations he can't handle, such as expecting him to share new toys or dress himself in five minutes.
- Plan ahead and watch for your child's signals. Don't shop when your toddler is tired, hungry or already cranky.

- Step in if your child is very frustrated (before it turns into a temper tantrum). Show her how to work her way out of the situation. Tell her what a good effort she is making in trying to in solve the problem.
- Watch for the signs of a tantrum. Make changes in the situation before a tantrum starts. If you see signs of a meltdown, you may need to cut the trip short, change what your child is doing, put the frustrating toy away, or make another change.
- Help him learn to recognize the signs, too. Teach him some words to say to let you know he's had enough. "I'm tired," for example. Then listen to him when he tells you!

Coping

If you missed the signs and can't prevent a tantrum, here are some things to try. One important thing to remember is not to lose your own temper. That won't solve anything!

- Pick up your child, and take her to a quiet place.
- Try holding your toddler until he can regain control of himself.

- If baby is overtired and out of control, put her to bed. Don't just leave her though. This isn't a "punishment." You're doing it to help her regain her control. Sit with her for a few minutes, gently rub her back and do other things from your bedtime routine to help her settle down.
- Some children may want to be alone. If your's does, find a quiet place for him to sit. Let him know you're near to help if needed.
- Show her how to work off anger (stomp her feet, punch a mattress, kick a pillow).
- Don't try to bribe your child to stop a tantrum. It won't work. Your child is feeling angry, frustrated and out of control. He needs to release the feeling, but you don't want to reward the behavior.
- Don't worry about what others are thinking when your child has tantrum. They've probably been there, too. As long as you're reacting calmly, firmly and with love to the tantrum, you have nothing to be embarrassed about.

149

Ready To Go: Helping the Babysitter

Most parents find that they need to leave their children once in awhile. Before you can go, you need to find a trusted babysitter. Everyone benefits when parents take time to prepare the babysitter and the child. Here are some things to talk about and write down before you leave.

For the sitter...

General information
- Your whole name, address and the phone number of your home or wherever your baby and sitter are. She may not know this or forget it in an emergency.
- Where you will be (name, address and phone) and when you will return.
- Emergency numbers—who, how and when to call for help. If necessary, talk about the location of the nearest pay phone and money for any calls.
- What to do about safety, emergencies, etc.
- Information about any medication that needs to be given and location of first aid supplies.

House information
- How to work appliances, fire extinguisher, etc.
- Location of light switches, light bulbs, thermostats, etc.
- How to lock doors and where to find keys.
- Peculiarities—tricky toilets, funny noises and other things that may cause questions or concerns.

Food
- Your expectations about cooking, meals and snacks—what, when and where.

Clothing
- Where clean clothes and pajamas are found.
- How baby should be diapered, where supplies are at and how to clean up when done.

Comforting, guidance and discipline
- Ways your baby likes to be helped, ideas to try that have worked best for you and others.
- Your baby's typical behavior and a bit about the developmental stage of your child.
- Behavior that requires discipline as well as behavior that does not.
- Methods to use and not use. Explain some details of how you do the comforting, guiding or disciplining.
- Talk about special toys, games, snacks that baby likes.

Routines
- Explain about special routines that baby expects and that help him. What, when, how and why you and baby follow the routines for bedtime, bathtime, mealtime and maybe other times.

Other expectations and rules
- Child: snacks, activities, behavior, bedtime, etc.
- Sitter: phone, TV, homework, food, visitors, cleaning up, etc.

And for your child...
- Help your child and babysitter get warmed up to each other before you go.
- Have the sitter meet your child a day or so before you need to be gone.
- Have the sitter come a little early so you have time to explain things and so baby gets to see that you are comfortable with and trust the sitter. Rushing out the door right away is scary for kids when they aren't used to a new babysitter.
- Consider a special plaything or activity for the sitter to do with baby.
- Let your child know that you are leaving—sneaking out is not fair. But, be careful not to overdo the "good-byes." Be brief, upbeat and loving.

Babysitter's Checklist

Child(ren) Name/age: _____

Parent's Name: _____

Home Address: _____

Phone (of home): _____

Nearest pay phone, if necessary: _____

Place parent will be: _____

_____ Phone: _____

Time of return: _____

Emergency: **Call 911 first.** (911 calls made from a pay phone are free.)
Then, call parent.

Someone parent trusts to help babysitter with a problem:

Name _____ Phone: _____

This person is a: ❏ Family member ❏ Friend ❏ Neighbor ❏ _____

Doctor:

Phone: _____ Medical record number: _____

Medicine: Who _____ What _____

When _____ How much _____

Other _____

Meals: When _____ What _____

_____

Snacks: When _____ What _____

_____

Naptime: When _____ Where _____

Routine _____

Bath: When _____ Where _____

Routine _____

Bedtime: When _____ Where _____

Routine _____

Other: _____

_____

Books and Babies

For Babies

- It's not too early to start reading to your child! Hold him on your lap and read for just a few minutes. When he starts squirming, stop.

- Start with books that have pictures of things that are familiar to your baby. You can make your own books with pictures from magazines, family photos or your own illustrations.

- Get or make a couple of sturdy "board books" that your baby can handle himself—and chew on if he wants. Babies still learn a lot through their mouths at this stage!

- Making reading time a quiet time helps your baby learn to focus. Turn off the TV and music.

- Encourage others to give your child books as gifts. Hand-me-downs are great. Keep books on a low shelf or in a special "book box."

For Toddlers

- Keep your toddler's books simple. Good books have clear, uncomplicated pictures.

For Moms and Dads

Your child wants to be just like you. If you want your little one to grow up with the advantages of being a reader—be one yourself. Let your child see you read newspapers, books, cereal boxes and more! If reading is difficult for you, consider contacting your local library or school to learn more about tutoring, classes and reading material written at a level you might find comfortable.

- Let your toddler set the pace for how long you stay on each page. It's also OK to "read" the book from back to front, if she wants to.

- Many toddlers want to start turning the pages. That can be his job when you read together. It helps him develop coordination. Remember: thick pages make the job easier.

- Start the routine of reading. A book or two at bedtime is a good way to make bedtime more popular for even the most reluctant sleeper.

- Two-year-olds love pointing to objects in the pictures and naming them. Encourage them!

- Toddlers are ready to see that pictures represent something else that is real. For example, a drawing of a cat represents a real, live cat.

- Read with expression. Use different voices for different characters.

- Toddlers are ready to choose their own books when you're reading together. You may get really tired of certain books, but when your child has a favorite, she'll want you to read it again and again and…!

- Choose stories you like, too. Don't read books you hate. (If one really drives you up a wall, maybe it can "disappear!")

For Preschoolers

- Three-year-olds like their books comfortable and familiar instead of scary and exciting (many start asking for "scary" as they near four years old).

- Stories about everyday life, families and animals are always popular. Some preschoolers will start getting interested in ABC and counting books.

- Story time keeps getting longer. That's good. Her attention span is getting longer.

- Stories can become more complicated. Preschoolers are able to follow a simple story.

- Give your preschooler more and more opportunity to "read" the story to you.

- Make reading fun! Find a good time—when you're both in a good mood—to read.

Choosing Children's Books: Which Book Is Best?

Here are some questions to ask yourself as you look at children's books. No book is perfect. The bottom line is—did you and your child enjoy the book? That's what makes a good book.

Pictures
- Can you enjoy the book for its pictures?
- Do you and your child like the illustrations?
- Do the pictures make sense? Do they go with the story?
- Do the illustrations or pictures represent all people fairly and respectfully? Do they avoid stereotypes?

Story
- Is the story simple enough for your child to understand?
- Is it too long, too short, just right?
- Is there a simple, satisfactory ending—a happy ending?
- Does the story match your values, beliefs?

Language
- Is it in the child's language?
- Does it use words kids enjoy—perhaps rhymes, silly sounding words?
- Can your child understand the words, ideas and concepts in the book?
- Is there familiar language that is colorful, flows easily and simply?

Matching Book to Child
- Will it enrich your child's life, excite the imagination and arouse curiosity?
- Does the book support your child's firsthand experiences?
- Are the characters real, unique and memorable?
- Do you like the book?

Other Things to Look For
- Repetition (I like apples, I like cats, I like…), rhymes or catch phrases.
- Familiar settings and events.
- One main character that is easy to identify with.
- Plenty of conversations. Avoid long paragraphs and descriptions until your child's attention span has developed.
- Bright, colorful, clear pictures that fit with the action and the story.
- Books can help children learn about themselves. For example, will the book help your child see how she is like other children? Or how she is unique and special? Both ideas are important to learn.

How to use Your Public Library: What a Deal!

Certainly one of the greatest institutions in American life is the public library. Almost every community has a library to use free of charge. Find the one closest to you and sign up for a library card. Take your child to the library, too. Many have programs for children, even very young "lap babies."

Getting a Library Card

In most libraries, to get a card you need only to present something that has your current address on it (a utility bill, drivers license or lease, for example). Your library card allows you to take many of the library materials home with you. Some things, usually called "reference books," have to stay in the library for librarians and others to use to answer questions.

Library Policies

Each library system (group of libraries in a city or community) has its own set of rules, such as: how long a book can be checked out, whether it can be renewed, what the fines are for materials returned after the due date, and how many books you can take out at a time. Ask about your library's rules.

What's There?

Most libraries have collections of books on almost any topic. Books are divided into two categories: fiction (stories, novels, poems, etc.) and nonfiction (how-to books, history, parenting, science, etc.). They may be separated into books for adults and books for children.

Libraries usually have collections of magazines for children and adults on many different topics. The newest copies generally stay in the library, older copies can be checked out.

Libraries may have videotapes (both educational and entertainment), tapes, CDs, games, toys, etc. Some libraries have photocopiers, computers and Internet access that you can use for free or a small fee. Not all libraries have these items. Check with yours to see what's there.

Finding It

Libraries try to organize their materials in a logical way to make it easy for people to find what they need. Nonfiction books are arranged by subject and usually assigned a number which tells what the subject is. This number is used to put the books in order on the shelves.

Fiction books are usually in order by author's last name and then by title. Libraries often have separate organization systems for biographies (books about people's lives) and nonbook materials.

(continued)

154

Finding It
(continued)

In the olden days, before about 1970, almost all libraries used catalog cards as a way to find their materials. Each item had a series of cards which were filed in different places in the catalog drawers so that library users had several ways to find a particular book. Now, many libraries have this information on computer. The computers are fast and usually easy to use.

Librarians are great sources of information and help. They can teach you to use the library catalog (whatever its form), find materials for you, suggest places to look for information, and generally make using the library easier. Don't hesitate to ask a librarian for help.

Many libraries create lists of books on different topics. Ask if your library has any. You may find lists of children's books on different topics, subject lists of books (such as cookbooks), or lists which complement special holidays or events (for example, Dr. Martin Luther King Day or starting school).

Children's Programs

Almost every library offers special programs for children. There are story hours for toddlers and preschoolers, summer reading clubs, book discussion groups and more. Some libraries offer programs for parents while their kids are in story hour. Librarians can recommend children's books, too. Look into what your library has for children. Find out when your child can get her own library card. Many libraries make this a special event—and it is. A library card can be the key to the world.

© Meld 1999 • 612-332-7563

TV and You

The TV is often part of baby's life even before he can really understand what's going on. Families use TV as entertainment, a babysitter and as a way to keep kids occupied. Really look at the issue of TV in your house so you can make decisions about your child and TV.

Know Your Baby

- Some kids are drawn to TV more than others. These kids may need more guidance in TV watching.

- Don't assume kids aren't "watching" TV just because they aren't looking at it. They absorb a lot from just being near when the TV is on. Know where your child is when you are watching shows that aren't appropriate for kids. Even young babies are affected by the noise, lights and sound.

- Toddlers are making great intellectual strides. Indiscriminate TV watching can interfere with development if it takes the place of other things to stimulate imagination, language and more.

- Children often act out the behavior they see on TV—good and bad.

- Understanding baby's temperament will help parents predict how she will react to certain shows. Use this and other knowledge of your child when making decisions about TV.

- Many children are too young to be able to understand subtle differences in the same kinds of shows. If cartoons are OK, then all cartoons are OK. They can't tell the difference between *Muppet Babies* and *Beavis and Butthead*.

Know Yourself

- Understand why **you** watch TV.

- Does watching TV interfere with other parts of your life—household chores, homework, family relationships, time spent paying attention to baby?

- How do you react to TV? Have you ever changed your behavior because of something you saw on TV—health issue, buying habits and more?

- TV can affect how adults look at crimes and other acts of violence. When we are bombarded with pictures of these things, we may start to think that violence is normal or become overly fearful of our surroundings. These feelings will be passed on to our children.

- Talk about the show and involve your toddler or preschooler in choosing what to watch. This helps them understand and follow your guidelines for watching TV.

Know the Situation

- TV watching can be affected by the situation—rules may change when baby or parent is sick, during holidays, bad weather or other times.

- Time of day often affects when the TV is on—the evening rush hour to get dinner ready is often a time for unsupervised TV watching. Early morning when you're busy and preoccupied can be another time.

- All TV is "educational" TV. It's teaching our kids something no matter what is on. Parents need to make sure that what's being learned is helpful, not useless or even harmful.

- TV watching may be different at others' homes. If Grandpa's favorite shows aren't OK for your child—too violent or scary—it can be hard to discourage him from watching them when your child is spending time with him. Talk to relatives/friends about your expectations for TV viewing, explain your reasons and ask for their cooperation when your child visits them.

© Meld 1999 • 612-332-7563

TV Time: Making Smart Choices

TV shows are aiming at younger and younger audiences. It can be so easy just to turn on the "tube" to keep a young child busy. Some families feel that TV watching can get in the way of learning, playing, conversation and family togetherness. Avoid some TV issues by making better TV viewing choices early on in your child's life. Here are some suggestions to try.

Have limits
Set time limits for how much TV will be allowed each day. Explain this to your child.

Watch by the show, not by the clock
If you allow two hours of watching each day, this doesn't have to mean turning on the TV at 3:00 pm and off at 5:00 pm. It may be a half-hour show in the morning, an hour after lunch and a half-hour of viewing in the evening.

Plan ahead
Use resources like TV Guide or television listings in the newspaper to know what comes on when, instead of turning on and changing channels until something catches your eye. Be picky. Choose what you will allow your child to watch on TV. And be picky about what you watch, too.

Special time
Plan special times to watch TV with your child. Specials for holidays, programs of historic interest, nature shows and more can be used for family time together. Plan ahead.

Talk about it
Talk later on about certain shows—whenever it seems appropriate. "Remember on Mister Roger's Neighborhood when he sorted out and then counted all the blue socks? Should we do that?" Tell your child your opinion of the action or messages on the TV. If something looks unrealistic, say so. Or ask, "Do you think that could really happen that way?" Even young toddlers can understand that TV isn't "real."

Special interests
When friends, family or babysitters are in charge, explain what is OK and what isn't for your child to watch. Ask for their cooperation when the TV is on.

Build on your child's interest in a TV show
If your child shows special interest in something she's seen on TV, help her find ways to learn more about that interest. Get an atlas or globe and show how to use it to find China, go to the library for books about kittens, make a simple drum to beat out rhythms, visit the fire station in your neighborhood and more! Use TV to expand her world.

Know the shows
Read about them, ask others or check them out on your own if you are unsure about how appropriate a show is for your child.

Check reactions
Watch how TV may affect your child. Does he act bored, angry, active, creative after watching certain shows? Do you like the way that the show affects him? If not, say no to that TV program for your child.

Offer alternatives
Plan ahead and be prepared to suggest other interesting activities to TV. Read books, color pictures, make an obstacle course, stack blocks, sing, dance, play ball, pull out the playdough and more.

Plan TV into your life— don't plan your life around TV
We can choose what to watch, how much, and when to turn off the TV. We control the TV, it doesn't control us.

Choosing Child Care

Like so many other things in life, finding good quality child care takes effort and planning. Take time to plan for child care well in advance of when you will need it—even before baby is born if you will be going back to work or school soon after birth. If you wait until the last minute, you may have to settle for less than you want.

Most Communities Have Two Main Options for Child Care

Child care centers

This is where children are cared for in a group setting by adults who are trained in child care techniques and child development. Some child care centers are part of large chains, others may be only in one location, like a church or school. Child care centers are licensed by the state.

Home or family child care

Family child care providers use their own homes to care for children. Often, one or more of the children belong to the provider and she or he cares for several additional children from other families. Most states also license home-based child care providers.

Look for a licensed center or provider. Licensing is important because it means that the child care has met a set of established standards and is regularly inspected by the state. Be sure to check out the licensing of any child care provider—center or home—you're interested in.

There are other options for child care, including relatives, in-home care and drop-in centers. The guidelines for choosing these options is similar to choosing a child care center or home-based child care provider.

Where to Look for Child Care

Agency referrals

Local child care referral agencies are in most cities. Call them for a list of licensed providers.

Word-of-mouth

Ask friends, neighbors, relatives, church members and others for recommendations.

Ads

You can get a good idea of the number and types of child care centers and even some home providers by reading the ads in your local paper.

Your own neighborhood

Keep your eyes open for child care in your area. Churches and schools often house child care centers. Home providers may have a sign or card in their yard or window.

Questions to Ask A...

Child care center

- Hours of operation
- Ages of children
- Cost (including any late pickup fees)
- How long has it been in business?
- How many children is the center licensed to care for?
- What is the ratio of children to staff?
- What are the qualifications of the staff?

(continued)

- Do they have training in child care, child development, first aid and CPR?
- How long have the staff been there?
- What is the center's philosophy regarding child development, including discipline?
- Are meals served to older children? What is a typical menu?
- How are toys cleaned?
- How often are diapers changed? When are sheets in cots or cribs changed?
- What will baby do every day and who will decide?
- Are there set routines?
- What are the safety policies regarding outside visitors? Is the center secure?
- What is the policy for sick children?

Home-based child care provider

- How many children are in your care? How old are they? How often do they come?
- What child care related education have you had? Do you have infant CPR and first aid training?
- What is the provider's philosophy regarding child development, including their approach to discipline.
- How long have you been in business? Do you plan to be in business for the long-term?
- Is your home non-smoking?
- Is TV allowed? How much?
- Are meals served to older children? What is a typical menu?
- How often are toys cleaned?
- How often are diapers changed? When are sheets in cots or cribs changed?
- What will baby do every day and who will decide?
- Are there set routines?
- Where will baby sleep? Does each child have his or her own sleeping space?
- Would anyone else ever take care of your child—for example, if the provider had an emergency? Who are they and what are their qualifications?
- What is the policy for sick children?

- Does provider have backup child care to recommend if she is sick and must close temporarily?

What to Look for In a Visit

Child care center

- Do the children seem happy? Do they look reasonably clean?
- Are the play areas bright and clean? Is there natural light?
- Is there a good selection of age appropriate toys that encourage creativity and motor development?
- Is the center clean— check bathrooms and food area? How does the place smell?
- Is there a safe outdoor play area?
- Is the center child-proofed? Are there fire extinguishers and marked fire exits?
- Do you see first aid supplies?
- Watch the staff work with the children. Do they seem attentive to the children's needs?

When looking into child care for your baby, it's important to ask the provider for references and to call to check them out.

(continued)

Choosing Child Care *(continued)*

- What is the noise level? Happy kids make noise, but too much noise could be a problem. What kind of noise do you hear?

- Do the providers seem able to set limits for children? How do they resolve conflicts between children?

- Does the staff seem willing to talk with you? Do they seem interested in getting to know you and your baby?

- Are you meeting everyone at the center, especially anyone your child will come in contact with?

- What's your "gut" feeling about the place—if it just doesn't feel right, it probably isn't.

Home-based child care provider

- Is the house clean? Check the bathrooms and kitchen. Is there carpeting? Is it clean?

- Are there pets? How many and what kind? Do children interact with pets?

- How does the house smell?

- Is the house childproofed? You should see gates, outlet covers, latches, and other evidence of childproofing.

- Where will children spend most of their time? Is the area light, clean, have comfortable furniture?

- Do children seem to be happy and having a good time?

- Does the provider seem calm or tense when dealing with the kids and with you?

- Is there a safe outdoor play area? If not, where does the provider take the kids for outdoor play?

- Is there a good selection of age-appropriate toys that encourage creativity and motor development?

- Check sleeping/rest areas, too, for comfort and safety.

- What's your "gut" feeling about the place—if it just doesn't feel right, it probably isn't.

With Any Child Care, You Should Expect These Things

- Regular, open communication. You should get frequent and complete updates about baby's progress and problems. This keeps you informed and able to deal with problems.

- Open door policy. You should be welcome to visit at any time, even without telling them you are coming. Providers should accept a reasonable number of calls from parents about baby's well-being, especially if baby has separation anxiety or other problems.

- Honesty and commitment. Provider should tell you what happens, without covering up. They need to keep commitments they make, too.

- Agreement with parents' wishes. Parents and provider must be able to agree on issues of discipline, TV watching, food, toilet training and any other things. If provider can't accommodate parents' wishes, they need to be honest about it.

- Advance notice of any changes in schedules.

- No advice unless asked for. Providers shouldn't offer childrearing advice or criticism unless parents ask for help.

(continued)

© Meld 1999 • 612-332-7563

Choosing Child Care *(continued)*

Other Considerations

- Location: Is it convenient to home, work and/or school? Can you get to it by bus, walking or other ways?
- Fees: Are fees reasonable? Can you afford them. Is the provider eligible for state/county reimbursement, if appropriate?
- What will you do if the child care provider is unavailable during the hours you need child care or if your baby is too sick to go to child care?

Too Sick for Child Care?

Children in child care do seem to catch everything that comes around. One reason is that they are exposed to many children all the time—some of whom are sick. Ask your provider what makes a child too sick for child care. Here are some reasons to stay home:

- Temperature of 101° F.
- Diarrhea can be highly contagious, especially in infants.
- Vomiting is a sign that something is wrong.

- Pinkeye (conjunctivitis) is a highly contagious infection of one or both eyes. Call the doctor for eye drops; once you start the drops, she is no longer contagious.
- Rashes can be caused by many things. Some are contagious, like ringworm and impetigo. Call the doctor.
- Chicken pox is contagious until the spots scab over—about a week. Call the doctor if you suspect chicken pox.
- Don't take a sick child to child care. You wouldn't want other parents to, so you shouldn't. Have backup care for those sick days.
- Don't overreact to minor bumps. Kids do get hurt in daily play. As long as injuries don't happen a lot and you are satisfied that reasonable safety precautions are being taken, there's probably no cause to worry.
- Be reasonable in your demands. Yes, you do have a right to expect the provider to do as you ask, but you need to be reasonable in your requests.

Parents' Responsibilities

You have high standards for child care—and your should, but parents have some responsibilities, too.

- Be considerate. This means picking up and dropping off your child according to the agreed upon schedule. Call if you will be late or early.
- Pay on time. This is important, especially for the home provider. This is her job and she relies on your payments.
- Be flexible. The rules may be different at child care than the ones you have at home. Try to adapt to those that don't actually conflict with your values.

Successful child care is a two-way street. Both provider and parents need to talk about their expectations and then live up to the agreements. Doing this can be the beginning of a beautiful partnership.

Your Notes

You can use this page to make notes about things you've learned, questions you have, milestones reached, and more. It can be a record of some of the events in your life as a new parent—your dreams, memories, concerns, hopes, and plans. Or perhaps this is a place to write down and celebrate baby's changes, growth and development —that first tooth, first word, first step...

Remember...

*You are the
most important person
in your baby's life!*

Meld
parenting that works

Qty.	Title	$ Each	Total
	The Middle of the Night Book	$12.50	

Subtotal _____

Shipping & handling _____

MN residents add 6.5% sales tax _____

Total _____

Shipping & Handling

For orders subtotaling:

Up to $25	$5.00
$25.01 to $75	$7.00
$75.01 to $150	$9.00
Over $150	8% of subtotal

Please call for Air Delivery Services and International Delivery pricing.

All orders must be prepaid.

Most orders are shipped within 2 days from receipt of order (7 to 9 delivery days).

Call for quantity discounts!

Send book(s) to:

Name _____

Agency _____

Street address _____

City _____

State _____   Zip _____

Telephone _____

Email _____

Method of Payment:

☐ Check or money order payable to Meld

☐ Visa   ☐ MasterCard   ☐ American Express

Account No. _____

Exp. Date _____

Signature _____

Mail to:

Meld ◆ 219 North Second Street ◆ Suite 200
Minneapolis, MN 55401

You can also order by phone, fax or on our website!

612-332-7563   612-344-1959 (fax)   www.meld.org

Meld
parenting that works

Order Form

Qty.	Title	$ Each	Total
	The Middle of the Night Book	$12.50	

Subtotal _____

Shipping & handling _____

MN residents add 6.5% sales tax _____

Total _____

Shipping & Handling

For orders subtotaling:

Up to $25	$5.00
$25.01 to $75	$7.00
$75.01 to $150	$9.00
Over $150	8% of subtotal

Please call for Air Delivery Services and International Delivery pricing.

All orders must be prepaid.

Most orders are shipped within 2 days from receipt of order (7 to 9 delivery days).

Call for quantity discounts!

Send book(s) to:

Name _____

Agency _____

Street address _____

City _____

State _____ Zip _____

Telephone _____

Email _____

Method of Payment:

☐ Check or money order payable to Meld

☐ Visa ☐ MasterCard ☐ American Express

Account No. _____

Exp. Date _____

Signature _____

Mail to:
Meld ◆ 219 North Second Street ◆ Suite 200
Minneapolis, MN 55401

You can also order by phone, fax or on our website!
612-332-7563   612-344-1959 (fax)   www.meld.org